To'. Torique

Thankyou for The
Support! Stay
focused!
       God Bless!

Pass The Torch

*How a Young Black Father Challenges the
'Deadbeat Dad' Stereotype*

Revised edition

by
Jamiyl Samuels
& Tracy-Ann N. Samuels, MSW

DEDICATION

To my **Father,**

I would like to thank you for being there during the first ten years of my life. I believe you are a good man who made some bad choices. In many ways you have shaped the man I have become by being there and by leaving. When present you were someone I looked up to because of your sense of humor, how well you got along with others, your athleticism, your love and support. You laid a foundation for me in our brief time together. In your absence, I was left to understand very adult issues at a young age.

I learned that I did not want my own son to feel the way that I felt the day you left for good. I learned that I would take my time and not marry until I am certain I would not need to break up my family for another woman. I am happy to say that I have succeeded in finding true love in my wife and son, and as witness to the dissolution of your marriage and my fear of failure in the eyes of God, I pray that I remain strong enough not to make the same mistakes. Now that you are gone I wish we had more time together to rebuild our relationship. Although I remain with more questions than answers, I am glad we were able to reconnect however brief the moments.

Sleep in peace.

Love,

Your son

To all young Black fathers who continue to refute the imposed "deadbeat" stereotype by taking care of their children, keep up the good work.

While this book - and the thesis it was adapted from - serves as a catharsis for me, I have found that not getting caught up in bad company, not getting locked up or using drugs (unless that is part of your story and you overcame it to be a success), finishing high school, earning a college degree, and/or being great at a particular talent is the best revenge if you are a victim of an absentee father or people who do not believe you will succeed in life.

Do not let a bad situation dictate the outcome of your future. Flip the script and do you. Whether it is at work, in school, or in life, give the haters something to really be upset about: the fact that you made something of yourself the right way. If you feel good about yourself, you can inspire your children whether as a biological or social father.

Why make a name for yourself, use the one you already have.

That is your legacy. Build on it.

PREFACE

I am aware that there are and will be many opinions on the topic I have chosen to write about. What started as my graduate thesis, with all the research and re-writes that came along with it, has been expanded to a non-fiction work, including personal anecdotes of my young life. My zeal for extolling the virtues of responsible Black men became more than just a grade for me.

I realize this is a very controversial and incendiary issue. I am cognizant of the history of the paternal role in America and the world, however I have chosen to focus on my story from the mid-1980s to the present, a time when Hip Hop music, television and Hip Hop inspired film, very influential to me during the period after my father left, became more a part of mainstream American culture, and therefore more of a target for criticism and stereotyping. Hip Hop and fatherhood in the Black community have a lot in common.

With the help of my wife, who has a Master's degree in Social Work, every statement and commentary not dealing with my personal life has been researched to the best of my ability. I in no way claim to be an expert in the area of "deadbeat dads" as every man's situation is different, still with my past and my future linked so closely to the impact of fatherhood, I felt it necessary to give my informed opinion.

I have learned a lot in putting this work together. I hope my book does, however small, its part in continuing to shed light on brothers who are taking care of their responsibility as fathers and role models to kids. I do not know all the answers, I do know what I experienced in my life as the victim of an absentee father and a young boy turned man growing up with Hip Hop culture.

Thank you for reading.

Table of Contents

ACKNOWLEDGMENTS

IN LOVING MEMORY
OF MY DAD
NEVILLE "DAD-NEVILLE" SAMUELS
JULY 15, 1953 – APRIL 11, 2012
AND
MY UNCLE
CLIFFORD LLOYD SAMUELS
OCTOBER 19, 1946 – OCTOBER 13, 2013
AND
DOUGLAS LYALL LEWIS, SR.
AUGUST 17, 1943 – JUNE 5, 2014

Family: for creating all the memories that made it into this book. I love you all

All the unsung Black fathers doing their job regardless of recognition: I salute you

Tracy-Ann, Trey Amani, and Aja Emily Sandy Samuels: for being my voice of reason and inspiring me every day. I love you

Hip Hop: for being there to keep me occupied and creative

Everyone who purchases this book: thanks for the support

Reporters and members of the media who recognize the Black father in a positive light: thank you

Social media: thanks for the platform and those using it to spread the word

IT TAKES A LOT OF HARD WORK AND DEDICATION TO BE A GOOD
FATHER, SOME MEN PREFER VACATION

PROLOGUE

My dad is my hero.

I wanted to do everything he did. I wanted to shave just like him so I ran a manual razor across my bare chin taking off a couple strips of flesh with the sharp steel blades. The warm blood that ran off my face into the sink scared me, but did not deter me. One day I would grow the facial hair necessary to use that razor properly.

I wanted to drive just like him so while he washed the family car I would sit in the driver's seat, my feet unable to reach the pedals below, jerking the steering wheel from left to right like a real-life game of Pole Position.

One day I did drive for real. More than ten years away from getting my permit, albeit unintentionally, I managed to move the gear shift into drive. As the car started to roll, I was unsure of where it would take me. I felt a nervous feeling in my stomach as the vehicle moved further and further from the driveway and closer to the street. My dad quickly sprung into action opening the driver's side door, sticking his right leg inside and jamming on the brake. Just as suddenly as the car started rolling, it stopped. My dad moved the gear shift back to the park position ending my impromptu joy ride. The car was not moving fast enough as there was no force applied to the gas pedal.

My dad was my hero that day.

He saved me and, to a larger extent, saved himself because if anything would have happened to me my mom surely would have killed him.

My dad is my hero.

He ran track and field, I ran track and field. He was in a bowling league, I wanted to be in a bowling league and I was. Soon I had trophies to put on the mantle right next to my dad's bowling trophies.

My dad is my hero.

He had to know how much I looked up to him. He had to know how much he inspired me. He had to know how much I enjoyed being around him, watching cartoons, the Professional Bowlers Tour on ABC, Major League Baseball, and those Big Apple karate movies on Saturday afternoon on channel 5.

My dad is my hero.

I almost had his name. I was almost a junior, but my mom wanted me to have my own identity.

"One of you is enough," she would say.

My name is Jamiyl (pronounced Ja-meel). I was born in Brooklyn, New York and have lived there practically my entire life save for the two years I lived in Baltimore while attending Morgan State University. My family is of Jamaican descent, but my name means "handsome" in Arabic. This meaning and the validity of it in comparison with my physical appearance was a source of ridicule in my elementary school when discovered by my peers.

Even though my name was different, I still wanted to do everything like my dad.

My dad was my hero.

But one day he decided he did not want the job anymore. Let's be clear, taking care of a child is a full-time job. It may not pay you a weekly or bi-weekly salary. The payoff comes every time that boy or girl smiles at you, every time he or she calls you mommy or daddy, when he or she graduates from pre-school, grade school, middle school, high school and/or college and he or she is straining to find you in a crowd of parents, finally seeing you and flashing that proud smile that lets you know 'I did it' and it was all because of your love and support.

He worked until my elementary school graduation, but my dad did not want the job after that. It was sudden, but then again you are never prepared to lose a family member in that way. It would take me years to hear a reason (see: excuse). No single decision has ever altered my life so deeply.

CHAPTER 1

THE CYCLE

As my wife stood expecting our first child I wondered how I would be as a father? How would I feel? How would I respond to the responsibility?

At 1:50 p.m. on a Saturday afternoon, the 10th of March 2007 to be exact, my life changed forever, more so than on the 16th of July 2005 when I got married at age 26. That sunny day in March, Trey Amani Samuels was born in New York Presbyterian Hospital's Greenberg Pavilion making me a father for the first time.

Sure the decision to make a lifetime commitment to one person is a life-altering event, but the birth of a child changes your whole outlook on life. Nine months of anticipation, anxiety, doctor's visits, sonograms, morning sickness, cravings, fatigue, mood swings, and a baby shower lead to the unbridled joy of hearing the first cry of your newborn.

From the time my father walked out of my life, I told myself I would be a better one to my child. As early as 14 years of age I would often daydream of the day I would have my own children, even writing down their names (I wanted four, but then again I didn't have to give birth to them). On the 10th of March there were no more what ifs. As they cleaned the blood off of Trey (that was one of the names I wrote down so many years ago) and he weighed in at just below seven pounds, it was time to make good on the promise to myself.

****

My earliest memories of my dad were good ones. He was a handsome man (where do you think I got it from?) with broad shoulders. He had a full beard, a signature laugh, and although he wasn't tall in stature, standing only 5'8", he was colossal in my eyes. He was very athletic. Also born in Jamaica, my dad played football - also known as soccer to Americans - and ran track and field.

I would follow in my dad's footsteps by running my first track & field event when I was five. It was the sub-bantam division of the 100 meters. I can still remember that I was winning the race, but slowed up because I was so far ahead of the field it felt wrong to be winning by such a large margin. I let one person pass me and settled for a silver medal.

Competing in track & field ran in the family as my mother and aunt Cynthia participated in the sport as high-jumpers in high school and my sister Andrea as a sprinter for the independent Concorde track team. The coach of Concorde track team was the brother of my Uncle Barry (my dad's brother-in-law). That 100 meter race was my first official race as part of Concorde track club. I would go on to win and lose a lot of races in my track & field career, setting records in the long jump in my age group along the way.

The ironic part about my track & field career is that my best moments occurred when my dad was not present at my events. I am not sure if I was trying too hard knowing he was there, or if I was overcome by nerves, or a combination of the two. I definitely felt butterflies in the pit of my stomach, but that was commonplace whenever I was about to take part in a major event. However, when my father was at my races I didn't only lose, I lost badly.

One venue in particular was extremely unkind to me during those days: Randall's Island. Although I had set the record for my age group in the long jump, a record that would eventually be broken, I had never won a race there. It got to the point where I would have near anxiety attacks when I knew I had a race on that track. I still remember stepping into the Greek Coliseum-style stands, seemingly stretching a mile wide in a massive oval of concrete. The open space was intimidating enough, but add thousands of people to the seats and the prospect of controlling the angst enough to focus on a race was equally daunting.

One Sunday my anxiety really got the best of me. My stomach was a little uneasy. My pain was definitely induced by nerves, but I did not want to run my race. I thought I could say I had stomach cramps and be excused from running like taking a sick day from school. To use the school analogy, there was one thing wrong with my little plan to get out of running: I was already in the building.

When you're at school and you get sick you call your parents to pick you up. My parents didn't pick me up. That is to say I wasn't getting out of running my race. My coach provided his brand of tough love the only way he knew how:

"Suck it up!"

My dad, for his part, was a little more encouraging, but if pain was all in the mind, it was already made up that I didn't want to go out there. The fact that they were going to make me run caused me to go into a slight panic attack. My eyes started to water as I made my way onto the red-colored rubber track. My breaths became short and heavy as if I just gotten my butt whipped for doing something wrong and I was told to stop crying.

If I recall correctly the race was 400 meters which was one lap around the massive track. By the time the race began I was mentally defeated. All I thought about was not being there in that moment. As I rounded the second turn and first straightaway, I was so far behind I could hear myself wheezing. I was in a steady jog at this point, my feet moving still hoping someone would pull me off the track. It was so quiet it felt like I was running in an empty stadium.

As I came around the second turn, 50 meters from the final straightaway, I looked up towards the finish line. It seemed so far away. Everyone in the race had finished or was about to cross the finish line.

'Why am I still running?' I thought. 'The race is over.'

My thoughts were being drowned out by the wheezing that got heavier and louder. Suddenly, as I rounded the turn to the final straightaway, my legs gave out. I collapsed onto the infield grass in a heap. I couldn't hear anything around me. There were thousands of people in the stands, but all I could hear was my crying. At that point I did not know if I was crying from stomach pain or shame and embarrassment at the fact that I gave up on the race mentally and physically. I had never quit on anything before.

With my face buried in the grass sobbing wildly, I felt a hand grab my arm. I looked up, my face wet with tears of humiliation, and there was my dad. My dad came to get me. As he helped me up, I cried harder. He threw my left arm over his shoulder as I clutched my stomach with my right hand. By this point no one could tell me I didn't have cramps. I already quit on the race so I had to finish what I started. As I was helped down the straightaway by my dad, I could hear the crowd cheering. If I was on the Olympic stage this moment would've been comparable to 1992 Olympian Derek Redmond[1] although I never made it to the finish line and my actions were far from valiant.

As I left the track, I looked up to see my coach. The look on his face said it all. I had let him down, but I didn't care at that moment. I just wanted to go home. My dad didn't lecture me, he didn't yell at me. As a matter of fact, I don't think anyone mentioned my debacle at all. Ultimately I had defeated myself before I stepped on the track. I failed myself, my team and I looked like a quitter in front of my family.

The very next weekend I was back at Randall's Island to run another 400 meter race. I felt like a different person. I felt like I could take on the world. The basis of my newfound confidence was redemption for the previous week along with the fact that my dad was not there. When I overheard a conversation between my parents and learned he would not be able to make it to the track meet, I exhaled deeply. My dad made me nervous when it came to track & field. I wanted to do well so badly in front of him that I tried too hard sometimes. I put added pressure on myself, so much so that I drove myself crazy, thus the meltdown of the previous week.

---

[1] Derek Redmond pulled his hamstring halfway through the 400 meters at the 1992 Olympics in Barcelona, Spain. Rather than get carted off on a stretcher, Redmond got to his feet and chose to finish the race on one leg. Writhing in pain, Redmond was soon joined on the track by his father Jim who helped Derek finish the race in one of the most emotional sports moments in history.

Now I was brimming with confidence as I took the track. I looked at my coach who took his usual position at the side of the track by the starting line, stopwatch in hand. I appreciated that he didn't look disinterested in timing me after my failure last week. I focused my eyes on the official that would start the race. As soon as he shot the pistol, I took off. I was flying around the track. I felt alone on the far side, but this time it was because I was so far in front. I didn't hear anything but my own controlled breathing. As I made the turn nearing the point where I dropped out the week before, I looked toward the finish line, but I didn't look behind me, a cardinal sin in track & field because it distracts and slows the runner's momentum.

As I passed "ground zero" from the week before with no signs of quitting this time, I heard cheering from the crowd. For an instant I thought they were so impressed with the magnificent race I had run or I was approaching a record time, but then I realized none of these people knew me to be cheering for me like they were.

Suddenly I saw an image to the right of me with my peripheral vision. It was a violent blur of motion: arms pumping wildly, legs moving like pistons in an engine. The image became clearer as it got next to me. It was another runner. He had caught up to me. I relaxed a little too much believing I had victory in my grasp. At that moment I tried to regain the energy I started the race with. My arms and legs were moving as fast as I could muster, yet the other guy continued to slowly move in front of me. It was a race to the finish line that had the crowd abuzz.

I put up as good a fight as I could, but I ran out of track. I lost the race. I had committed another cardinal sin of track & field: I started too fast for the distance I was running and thus I could not finish as strong as my competitor for he had more in the tank than I at that point.

I immediately dropped my hands to my knees in an attempt to catch my breath. I was stunned. I thought I had the race won and I lost. I looked over at my coach expecting a look of disappointment. The smile that crossed his face was one I rarely saw during the heat of a meet. He looked at his stopwatch and back at me then walked away from the track.

I believe I ran that 400 meters in 73 seconds which might have been my best time ever at that distance. Sure it is a far cry from the 42 seconds of Olympic athletes, but I was eight years old. It was my record.

My coach was happy so I was happy. He was a hard man to please, a perfectionist. Sometimes you need people like that to challenge you to be great. The same can be said about being a parent. You have to challenge yourself to be the best parent you can be to your child so he or she can take those lessons and bestow them on his or her future family. It is a never-ending cycle that begins subconsciously through experience within a stable family structure.

There is no way at eight years old I am thinking about being the best father I can be to anybody's child. Heck, I did not even know how children came into the world yet, and I should not know at that age.

All I knew is that I ran the race of my life that Sunday and my dad missed it. I struggled with the irony of the situation. I was relieved he wasn't there because it allowed me to relax and ultimately do well, but what was the purpose if my dad couldn't share my greatest moments with me.

The day became a running joke with my coach. Before we left Randall's Island that evening, coach told my mother to tell my dad to stay home every weekend I have a race. Later that day, the shock on my dad's face when he was told what I did was priceless. I had made him proud even if he was not physically present and that went a long way in allaying my fear about whether I was letting him down by performing well in his absence.

I tell this story to make a point that even though my dad ultimately left us, he was not a demon. I choose to show his pleasant side in my anecdote because there is good in everyone. It was also what I was used to seeing from my dad. He seemed so calm at all times. I rarely saw him angry or argue with anyone. I saw him get along with everyone he came in contact with, qualities I have been told I possess. Which is why what my dad did was a total shock to me. I never saw it coming. It is easy to judge someone from the outside looking in, but circumstances dictate action in most cases.

Only three people know the cause of the moment that changed the dynamic of my family: my mother, my dad and God.

The way I cared about making my dad proud, I can only hope my son takes as much pride in doing well for me as he grows up. The way he looks at me and flashes that infant-toothed smile, I think I am off to a good start. It pains me to walk out of the door to go to work, pick up my wife, or go to the store and hear him run after me as I go out of the door.

It is why I can't fathom how some men so easily walk away from their children. In some cases it is not always the father's fault. Things happen. I can write ten books about how I can't see how people leave their kids and, God forbid, something can happen tomorrow where I would have no other choice but to do just that.

With that being said, I will explore all angles, exhaust all avenues, leave no stone unturned on this subject to not leave any Black father's situation out of the realm of possibility. One thing I know for sure, there is no doubt that there are some good brothers left.

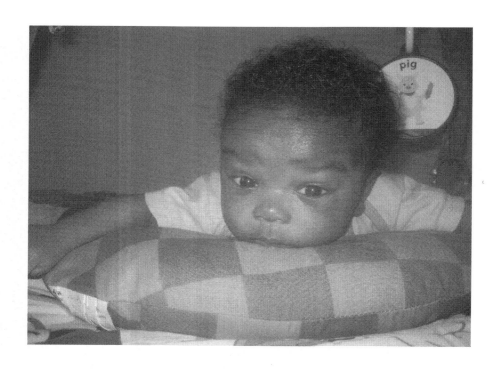

CHAPTER 2

"BE A FATHER"

"Be a father, if not, why bother, son/ a boy can make 'em, but a man can raise one..."[2]

I made the conscious decision to be in the delivery room for Trey Amani's birth. I wanted to be the first person my son laid eyes on when he took his first breath in the world. From the time of Trey's conception sometime at the end of June 2006 (although I cannot remember the exact day I remember the act and failed use of the withdrawal method), the subsequent 36 weeks or so was filled with trepidation. Once my wife Tracy-Ann confirmed a seed was planted, we only told a handful of immediate family: my mother, my sister, my mother-in-law, Tracy-Ann's grandmother and that might have been it. We wanted to make sure we got through the first trimester this time.

---

[2] Ed O.G. of rap group Ed O.G. & Da Bulldogs. *Be A Father To Your Child.* Roxbury, Massachusetts, 1991

At times I still can't believe I am a father. It is the ultimate act of selflessness to put someone else's well-being before your own. I soaked up every minute of impending fatherhood. The day we found out the sex of the child was especially nerve-racking. For years Tracy-Ann talked about wanting a girl as the first child. I didn't care what sex the child was as long as it was healthy. Well, that was only 90 percent true. While I wanted a healthy child, I secretly, or not so, desired a son. I say not so secretly because my wife knew of my wish. I even reasoned why it would be beneficial to have a boy first.

"He could look after his younger siblings," I said.

"Please," my wife shot back.

In my chauvinistic mind, I felt that the first child should be a boy. God may have other plans and I was preparing myself for that. We were at New York Presbyterian Hospital.

The efficiency of the faculty at New York Presbyterian was apparent from the first check-up. My wife was receiving top of the line care and today we would know if we would be buying baby blue or pink. What was I rooting for? Here's a hint: I'm a New York football Giants fan.

Adding to my anxiety was the fact that it was hell trying to park in Manhattan during a business day. I had to let Tracy-Ann out in order to find a parking space. That meant the procedure would start without me. By the time I got to the room she would know what she was having. This was crazy. At least the store Babies R'Us had parking for expectant mothers. Surprisingly, I was able to find a parking spot faster than usual. It was cruel irony.

The ubiquitous feeling of nervousness encompassed the pit of my stomach. My heart began to beat faster as I put my vehicle in park and removed the key from the ignition. I have long legs and thus the ability to walk very fast, but today it felt like I was gliding. From the car to the building to the elevator to the reception area I never moved so fast.

As I made the right turn into the room, Tracy-Ann was on her back with her stomach exposed covered in a clear gel. Drawn curtains dimmed the room. The attending nurse greeted me as I walked in. She moved the device that would allow us to see an image of the growing fetus gently across my wife's belly. I looked at the screen, searching for an answer to the million dollar question: was it a ball player or not?

"Come and look at your son," she said.

Although my outward expression betrayed little emotion, inside I was doing a Balki dance of joy[3]. I'm sure God heard the "thank you" I gave Him in my mind. I felt like He must have been tired of hearing my voice. I thanked God on many nights for allowing my family and me to see another day. I thanked Him for the gift of procreation and starting life in my wife's stomach.

---

[3] Actor Bronson Pinchot's (Balki) signature dance done with Mark Linn-Baker (Larry) from the classic sitcom *Perfect Strangers* (1986-1993).

I prayed for a healthy child, I prayed that my wife would have a healthy pregnancy, and I thanked Him for leading us to one of the best hospitals in New York. I know God doesn't make mistakes regardless if it is a decision you disagree with that is painful and feels like a loss. He always picks you up and is always on time. He felt 2007 was our time and I will never question that. Thank you, Lord.

I removed my hat and took a seat next to the bed and stared at the screen. I saw the shape of a small little body. I saw that from left to right on the screen the big circular object was the head. This was confirmed by the nurse.

She maneuvered the sonogram instrument with her right hand and pointed out different parts of the body with her left. I stole a quick glimpse at my wife who smiled proudly as she watched the screen. I could see she was at ease and that made me happy. As my eyes continued from left to right a small little shape pointing upward caught my eye.

"Here is the arm," the nurse would say moving her left hand along the screen at the image of a little arm that ended at the little shape that was pointing upwards.

"Oh my," the nurse exclaimed.

The nurse started to smile. She was hesitant to say what the sonogram was showing out loud.

"He's holding his penis?"

So my wife said it for her.

"That's normal," the nurse shot back.

"Lord, Jesus. Starting already, just like his father," Tracy-Ann joked.

My son was holding his pee pee…like a real man. I was glad he had something to hold. I was glad he was a he.

I wonder if my dad felt the same way when he knew that I was going to be a boy. Maybe at that point there was just relief that I was going to be healthy.

There is a nine year age difference between my sister and I. Even though we have different fathers that is still a big gap for two siblings. I brought this point up to my mother one day and she informed me that she had two babies that died at birth, both boys. The third time was the charm I guess.

I could have had two older brothers. The revelation knocked me for a loop. How different would my life have been with two males to look up to? Would it have been an easier transition with two brothers to comfort me? I will never know, but I found myself at times wishing my brothers lived so I could share things that guys share. They would have been older by the time my dad left.

Hell, my father probably would have never left at all. Maybe my brothers would have stopped him. I will never know.

****

Trey was not ready to come into the world as scheduled. 36 weeks had come and gone and Tracy-Ann was not even dilated. There were the requisite false alarms, one that had me scrambling from my hotel job as soon as I started my shift. After another few days with no signs of dilation, the decision was made to take the baby out by Caesarean section. Once a definite date was set the anticipation began.

The next few days leading up to Saturday were filled with sleepless nights, last-minute shopping and preparation for the birth of our child. I set up my paternity leave (I didn't know that existed for men until I was told of the option) from work and I was ready. Packing the hospital bag really brought it home that I was going to be a father in less than 24 hours. I looked back on everything in my life leading up to this point.

"Would I be a good father?" I thought.

Was I prepared mentally, physically, emotionally and financially for what was about to happen? All the preparation in the world can be done for an event, but you will never know how it will turn out until it happens and you are thrown full force into the fire.

All the diapers given as gifts from the baby shower will eventually run out. What then? Find that $35 for more. You can cram for a test and find out what you studied is not on the exam. What then? You make an educated guess. Life is not going to go according to your plan.

Preparation is good, but it is how you adjust and adapt to the changing situation that will define you. I believe this ideology applies to parenthood as well. I stopped worrying and overanalyzing. When the baby entered the world we would go from there.

The second Saturday in March was D-Day, or B-Day if you want to get technical. As usual my wife was up before I was, but I hopped out of bed when awoken (usually it is a slow painful process rolling out of bed for me – possibly a sign of old age). It was a sunny day (always a good sign) and the morning preparation and drive to the hospital went smoothly.

Upon reaching the hospital we went to the ninth floor of The Greenberg Pavilion where Tracy-Ann was checked in almost immediately. We had become familiar with this part of the hospital a week before when contractions that were close in proximity to each other gave a false sense of impending birth.

Today was a set date for Trey's arrival whether he was ready or not, so there were no qualms about whether to prepare Tracy-Ann for delivery. Truth of the matter is she wasn't even dilated, not even a centimeter. Trey was enjoying his warm safe haven in his mother's womb with no intentions of making an appearance any time soon.

I was given a powder blue cap and blue gown to cover my clothes with. I was so excited I started taking pictures of myself. I placed the digital camera on a table and set the timer for ten seconds, running to pose before the camera flashed. My smile was a mile wide and I felt the sudden urge to buy cigars.

I ran to Tracy-Ann's bedside, her belly still protruding from under the hospital attire she was given. I continued to take self-portraits of her and myself. My jubilant camera work irked my wife, who didn't like taking pictures unless she was well dressed. A clear cap and hospital garb was not her ideal uniform for self-portraits, but she decided to grin and bear it because of how giddy I was.

There was a medium-sized black and white clock on the far wall directly across from Tracy-Ann's bed. Once picture time was over, it was time to watch the clock. As various nurses moved in and out of the room performing mandatory diagnostic tests, it seemed like the big hand never moved on the clock; sort of like how I felt when I was in elementary school when I thought three o'clock would never come. We were given a window between 12:30 and 1:30 p.m. as to when the surgeon would bring Tracy-Ann into the delivery room. It was agonizing waiting for time to pass.

At a quarter past one o'clock a surgeon walked into the waiting room to tell us she was ready to proceed. A rush of nervous energy filled my stomach. It was time to deliver our baby and Tracy-Ann was more than ready if her face was any indication. One thing for sure her sense of humor was still intact moments before the biggest surgery of her life. Pressed for one last picture of her taking the last walk as an expectant mother, she still found time to move the hospital gown to the side and moon me as she walked towards the delivery room. Trey would not come out on his own, now the doctors were ready to reach in and grab him.

The delivery room was not like I imagined it, seeing so many on television shows like *The Cosby Show* and soap operas like *All My Children* and *General Hospital*. The room was like any other except for the scale used to weigh the newborn in one corner next to a small table. There was a bed in the middle of the room where Tracy-Ann was already on. Her body was split in half by a powder blue curtain. From the bosom down her belly was exposed and she was surrounded by doctors and surgeons in white uniforms.

Our obstetrician was in full white medical doctor garb with the white mask over her face. The other staff in the room served various functions. One prepped Tracy-Ann's belly for the Caesarean section, the other ladies were in charge of cleaning up and weighing Trey after he arrived. She had already been given a huge needle called an epidural.

An epidural, as many women will tell you, is a vital drug administered into the spine used to numb the lower region of the woman's body in preparation for delivery.

I heard stories about the epidural needle, but I had never seen one up close. I never cried when I got stuck with a needle as far as I can remember, excluding infancy of course. Blood work during mandatory doctor visits as a preteen was tear-free. Even when I needed stitches in my mouth after taking an ice ball to my face during a seventh grade snowball fight I took the huge needle used to apply anesthesia with a hum, to my aunt's surprise.

However according to my wife, nothing compares to the size of this needle. She hates needles so I imagine her back was turned when the doctor pulled it out. I think I would panic just seeing an epidural needle let alone having someone stick it in my spine. I definitely have a greater appreciation about what a woman goes through to bring life into this world.

I was positioned right next to Tracy-Ann behind the blue screen, surely better for my stomach not to see her insides out in the open. Looking in her eyes I saw a mix of nerves and anxiety. It had been a long nine months and at this point she wanted to get it over with. A male doctor, not the lead surgeon, let us know what to expect once the baby was out. As he spoke, my mind began to race a mile a minute. I began to get the nervous feeling anticipation brings. I was a few short moments from seeing my newborn son.

"What would he look like," I thought to myself.

Looking back, and I may get struck down for this, at the time I secretly hoped the baby wouldn't be ugly, a punishment for making fun of so many babies who were less than attractive. I had so many things running through my head that I was ready for it to be over.

I held my wife's hand as the surgeons prepared to cut her open. Tracy-Ann stared at the ceiling and I watched her waiting to hear the first sound from our baby. After what seemed like an eternity, in reality probably five minutes, we could hear the surgeons commenting about the baby.

"Alright here it comes," one surgeon said.

"He's beautiful," said another.

The surgeons continued to gush over our newborn, yet we were a prisoner of our suspense behind the curtain, yet to hear a sound from the baby.

"Why isn't he crying?" my wife wondered.

At that moment I thought of all the television dramas of newborn deliveries where the baby comes out blue in the face or with the umbilical cord wrapped around the neck. Call me a pessimist, I can take it. I don't know why I happen to think the worst at times. Although there was not an iota of panic in the voices of the surgeons, the anxious first-time parents trapped behind the blue wall did not hear a sound. Either they were still in the process of pulling him out or they had not cleared his nasal and oral passages.

Whatever was going on I was getting impatient. Suddenly the silence was broken by the sharp cry of the smallest person in the room. It was a beautiful sound. As abruptly as it came, it was gone. It was official: the verbal confirmation that I was responsible for another life; life made possible by the miracle of procreation, the beauty of fetal development, and the strength of the woman carrying our child.

"Here he is," said a nurse holding the smallest, precious pink-colored package. We had come face to face with our boy staring back at us with what seemed to be jet black eyes. He looked like an alien to me at that moment. Just as swiftly as he appeared, he was gone; off to get cleaned up. I looked back at Tracy-Ann still feeling the shock of officially becoming a father.

"Dad, get over here," called one of the nurses.

I immediately jumped up, believing that I was to remain behind the curtain the entire time. I saw two nurses, one with glasses and another without (it was the only way I could differentiate between the two as they both had on all white from head to toe), bringing Trey to a table next to the scale.

"Where's your camera?" the nurse without glasses quipped. "You gotta be on the ball, dad. This is the time to take pictures."

Indeed the shutterbug had put his camera away believing I could not take pictures in the delivery room. I don't know why I thought that, seeing so many shows where proud fathers videotape the birth of their children. Given the go-ahead to take pictures I immediately pulled out my digital camera and, with the record function, captured Trey's first real cry. I was emotional, though I did not shed tears. My voice cracked as I whispered his given name out.

Trey once again stopped crying after the initial wail prompting the nurse to lightly shake him a few times before laying him back down on the table to clear his nostrils and mouth of any remaining mucous. He cried again as the nurses continued to clean him up. I couldn't help but notice how rough the nurse without glasses was handling Trey.

I understand that she probably handled thousands of newborns in a similar fashion, but that didn't ease my concern. She grabbed his legs and lifted him off the table, flipped him, wrapped him in a series of swift movements. I wanted to tell her to be careful, this was not IHOP.

Against my better judgment I took a peek - more like a look triggered by my peripheral vision - over at the operating table and quickly regretted it. In the nanosecond I looked and looked away I had already seen more than I wanted to.

There was blood everywhere as the surgeons feverishly worked to basically stuff my wife's organs back into her stomach. This was a delicate process (maybe feverishly is a bad choice of words) that would determine if she would be able to use the bathroom normally for the rest of her life. No pressure.

Trey Amani Samuels weighed in at almost seven pounds. Once his tiny feet were inked up and stamped on the white piece of paper containing his vital stats, he was ready to meet his mommy. Predictably fussy after getting pulled into the real world from his warm amniotic sac and flipped like a "Rooty Tooty Fresh n' Fruity" special, Trey was brought over to his mother wrapped in an all-white hospital issued blanket. Only his face was visible as he was carefully placed on my wife's chest. One word from Tracy-Ann and Trey stopped crying and blinked his ointment-covered eyes at his mommy as if he recognized her voice from the countless days of talking, reading, and singing to him while in her womb. It was a beautiful moment, one that I captured on camera.

Shocking, I know.

CHAPTER 3

A BLACK FAMILY

My father's actions qualify him as a "deadbeat dad" in the court of public opinion. If you ask me at the time I did not think he was a deadbeat at all. I didn't even know what that meant. He tried to keep in contact with me until it was made impossible to do so without coming back home. I definitely gave him the benefit of the doubt.

Still there was a home to come back to for another year and two months. Just show up at the door, apologize and all would be forgiven. There were other issues, apparently, between him and my mother that were so irreparable that he did not want to return. All I knew is that I was waiting for my father to come home and he never showed up.

I don't think all the adjectives in the world could describe how I felt, but here are a few: unwanted, dejected, confused, sad, angry.

The longer he stayed out there and his family was not receiving any emotional or financial support, my father willingly put himself in a category: a card-carrying member of the stereotypical Black father club. I guess I should be thankful he stuck around through the 1980s at least.

Between 1984 and 1990 crack addiction became a nationwide epidemic. Hundreds of thousands of Black people in particular succumbed to violence and drug abuse. There were reports of abandoned babies, babies born under the influence of drugs and kids being placed in foster homes. Black women were raising multiple children by themselves having to rely on public assistance to make ends meet.

Crack-related criminal activity was almost always the lead story on the evening news with the backdrop of a predominantly low-income neighborhood littered with broken liquor bottles, crack vials, and vacant lots (take a look at the video for *"The Message"* by *Grandmaster Flash and the Furious Five* for further visual evidence of the type of community most immediately affected).

However there were other reasons besides the crack epidemic why Black fathers were missing from their children's lives; incarceration (possibly because of drug use or possession), the father may not be aware of the child's existence, or the mother may be using the child as leverage against the father for one reason or another purposely keeping him or her away. These are all valid scenarios including the most prevalent one: the father (whether it be a teenager, or young adult who engaged in irresponsible sexual activity) is either too scared, or (a grown man who thinks he's too cool to take on the responsibility) has no interest in being a parent so he cuts and runs out on the family he helped create.

Thankfully I was fortunate enough not to experience these real world problems as my environment was decidedly middle class. While I did not live in the suburbs by any stretch of the imagination, my childhood was free from exposure to the dangers of drugs and criminal activity. My mom worked as a certified nursing assistant and my father was an electrician.

I didn't really want for anything. We did not fall on hard times. We lived on the second floor of a modest private house on East 32nd Street between Snyder and Tilden avenues in Brooklyn New York. I went to one of the best public schools in Brooklyn at the time: Public School 235.

My father had excuses for leaving us behind, some of which I would learn years later, but to me there was not a valid one at the time because we were much better off than some of the Black families struggling to survive on a daily basis. I learned abandonment can happen to anyone regardless of economic background.

On the flipside, many young Black men work hard to be a pillar of stability in their children's lives. One of my best friends growing up had both of his parents present. I met Douglas Lewis, Jr. in the second grade and we became real cool. Even as a child I had a keen sense of people. Although I'm a friendly person by nature I only consider a chosen few to be my close friends. Like, I-know-their-immediate-and-extended-family-and-vice-versa close. I wish I could divulge the process of how or why I decide these people would be a part of my inner circle, but I have no idea myself. It is not something I can say I think about it just happens over time.

Douglas Lewis Sr. was someone I can say I looked up to growing up - not because he allowed me into his home at all times of the day and night as I speed walked the 15 blocks from my home to play Nintendo with his son (Junior had all the best sports games) - because he always smiled. He was easy going, his hair was impeccable (his afro was always neatly trimmed – I mean never a hair out of place), and he had the type of cars that when they drove by your street you were pointing to it with a group of kids yelling "that's my car"! Most importantly he, along with his wife (one of my second mothers), was an example of true love and stability. I never saw them argue. Although I'm sure there were days that things did not go well they never appeared to let it affect their overall spirit. It was what I was used to seeing at home.

They were a model of consistency. Even when my family portrait fractured, there they were in the same house, dad walking along Avenue D to get his hair cut, flashing that winning smile whenever he saw me. There he was, retired from working yet taking it upon himself to drive to the other side of Brooklyn, sitting outside of the hospital where his wife was employed waiting to pick her up after a long day of work…every day.

There was the time I was walking along Avenue D and saw them jogging together. I did not know it then (I thought it was cute), but seeing these two people, married over 30 years at that point, in their 60s taking the time to work out together was amazing. It may seem trivial, but it was something they were doing together. They were with each other. That is what mattered.

Douglas Lewis Sr. passed away in 2014. It hurt my heart because you think a man like him would live forever. I dedicated a poem to him at his wake. It was my tribute. It was the least I could do, but it did not feel like enough. Douglas Jr. remains a solid individual. A guy I witnessed on numerous occasions forego alcoholic beverages for bottled water at a club. A man who inherited his dad's love for cars. I can only attribute his great character to the man whose name he bears.

On the other hand, another of my friends had the namesake of his father, but chose to use his middle name. I only knew him by his middle name and never saw his father in the home where he lived. Like me, his parents were separated before he was a teenager. Children will always make a statement when they are hurt. The impact of a father cannot be understated.

I think back to the images of the Black family that was on television when I was growing up in the late '70s and early '80s, shows like *Good Times*, *The Jeffersons*, and *The Cosby Show*. These were low, middle and high income Black families that laughed together and cried together. Although the Evans family struggled on *Good Times*, despite all the frustration trying to provide for his family, the patriarch James never thought about leaving. James Evans, Jr. (J.J.), the star of the show, was a wisecracking artist proud to have his father's name.

No matter how many times George and Louise argued on *The Jeffersons*, they remained together. They had a committed marriage that stood the test of time - and their maid Florence. The show also explored rare network television terrain at the time by having George's best friend Tom be a White man who was married to Helen, a Black woman.

These were strong Black men that when we laughed at them it wasn't to keep from crying at a negative or stereotypical portrayal. They were the undisputed head of the household and they were relatable to the Black audience. Where are the images of a Black family on television today? Since the ABC hit sitcom *Family Matters* went off the air, television has dissolved into a mix of reality shows ranging from competition (*Survivor*, *The Biggest Loser, The Bachelor*), cooking (*Iron Chef*), fashion design (*Project Runway*), teenage pregnancy (*Teen Mom*), and drug rehabilitation (*Celebrity Rehab*).

While the aforementioned shows relay a strong message to a specific audience, the real question is why are people obese, getting pregnant in their teens and becoming addicted to drugs and alcohol? Because there is probably no support system to prevent these issues from happening. In this age of new technology where a phone comes out and quickly goes out of style when the newer version is introduced two months later, people are forgetting how to hold a conversation with one another.

One powerful Black reality program that caught my attention was *Toya's Family Tree*, but even on that show the father makes a cameo appearance yet he is noticeably absent from the family and the fallout is played out in every episode.

Whether Toya and her brothers were escorting their drug-addicted mother to the rehab facility or the youngest brother Rudy was lashing out at a father he never really knew, the program showed how drugs and abandonment destroyed families.

Tyler Perry's House of Payne was a well-received show centered around the Black family, but it flew under the radar airing on TBS. Even more so for people that could not afford cable television to watch BET or TBS. We need these types of shows back on network television. Kids need to see a loving Black family on the small screen.

Personally I am glad that I was too young to know much about stereotypes as they related to the Black community. Then again growing up in the 1980s there was no internet, cell phones were not advanced to touch screen status and unable to deliver news alerts, very few people had cable television (I was lucky if we got more than rice grains with the old WHT setup my father brought into the house), and I did not care much for the evening news beyond the sports report.

Today, kids can get a hold of a lot of information - damaging, salacious and otherwise – very easily. Too much information can be dangerous in the wrong hands. Too many kids do not know or understand the history of racism, yet may experience it on a website or in school.

Worse yet, a lack of home training or healthy reinforcement and self-awareness by parents may allow a lot of Black kids to feed into the racial stereotypes by participating in ignorant public behavior such as using vulgar language loudly on public transportation, disrespecting elders, and/or dressing provocatively (girls) or with their pants pulled down to their upper thigh (boys).

Kids my age were rowdy as were those the generation before me and so on, however I cannot recall so many instances of a jailhouse mentality (pants hanging low is symbolic of jailed criminals in a chain gang who cannot wear belts in prison) in so many Black kids.

A lot of these young men are imitating the way Hip hop artists wear their clothes on stage. As I will state many times, Hip Hop was a major influence on me and the artists I grew up listening to were promoting Black power, female empowerment, and curtailing violence, along with their traditional boasts of great lyricism. The fashion trends of the time were relegated to hair styles and name brand clothing. I can't remember KRS-One, Rakim, Big Daddy Kane, A Tribe Called Quest, or NWA for that matter wearing their pants off their waist. LL Cool J had his shirt off practically all the time and his pants were always at a respectable level.

Hip hop thrived when it was creative and cutting edge. A current Hip Hop superstar needs to do something innovative like not showing their underwear when they walk around. Who knows it may start a movement in the other direction.

These kids need to know that they are not carrying themselves in a mature fashion. I am aware it is easier said than done, but a young man who chooses to follow what they see someone else do may have some underlying self esteem issues. Confidence is a positive word or action away. Why follow someone else when you can make your own statement?

As Black men became more scarce in the lives of their children, the anger and resentment pent up in the kids left behind made it harder to control deviant behavior. How is a child going to learn self respect and how to respect others when he or she was disrespected by the father who chose to walk away?

I tried to stay away from starting trouble with anyone for no good reason. I was angry at my father not the guy on the street. I always believed if you looked for trouble it would find you. Wanting to stay away from conflict did not make me a punk, it made me stay alive.

One of my first jobs, ironically, was that of a recreational assistant to the elderly and a peer counselor for the Youth Health Corps. I was taught at a young age to respect my elders and helping the elderly feel some enjoyment during their day while absorbing their wisdom was a great experience for me. To see kids fighting older women on public transportation and (along with some adults) failing to give their seat to the elderly or a pregnant woman breaks my heart. These common courtesies are learned in the home.

Being a peer counselor in the summer youth program was the most fulfilling because I was able to spend my summer productively being creative, improvising skits on health and family issues such as drug abuse, teen pregnancy, HIV/AIDS and sexual abuse, performing and informing pre-teens (one little girl gave me her only piece of candy after a performance), and getting paid ($4.25 an hour at that time).

I felt like I was making a difference in another child's life. I wasn't sulking or feeling sorry for myself and my father never crossed my mind. Unfortunately the year I went away to college was the same year they shut down the Youth Health Corps, but more community programs are needed for at-risk youth. Positive mentors and outlets are needed to earn the respect of inner city kids who feel unwanted and discouraged by selfish acts of abandonment.

Unfortunately advanced technology is making verbal communication practically obsolete. You can't see a person's facial expression or hear the sincerity, or lack thereof, in the voice through texting.

In no way am I condemning texting. It is a wonderful advancement and necessary tool in business and it is a convenient way to reach a friend or loved one quickly, especially if they live out of town.

There still needs to be a balance. Remember pay phones? Hardly see them on the street nowadays, in New York at least. When I had my own pager light years ago I couldn't pull out a cell phone when I got a beep. Leaving a voicemail was how you "texted" back in the day if you couldn't reach someone, but at least your voice was heard. Now those quiet moments when you would normally pick up the phone and call a dear friend or relative or even go visit them in person, are replaced by the inclination to turn on the computer or grab a cell and text.

I am guilty of this at times as well. The issue becomes way more disturbing if the parties in question are parents and children. Technology should never take the place of conversation with kids. A young boy or girl locked in their room on a computer while the adults are in another room without bothering to check in on what the child is doing can be a recipe for disaster. This disconnect is just as bad as leaving the home in my opinion. Dare I say, it is okay to nag your children. Let them know what you will not tolerate and monitor their online and phone usage. You will not be their favorite person at the time, but they will know you care about what they are doing.

My mother always wanted me to give her the number of any friend's house that I was staying at. I made sure I was where I said I was for fear she would call to check up on me. It wasn't that she was keeping tabs on me, but my mother felt better knowing where I was going to be and who I was with.

I recall reading an interview on Hip Hop star Busta Rhymes where he lamented about a guy who texted him even though he was in the same building in the room next door. It takes nothing to walk to the next room and speak face to face.

There is something about hearing a person's voice, seeing a person in the flesh that cannot be duplicated through texting. The introduction of Skype and Face Time on the iPhone is a step in the right direction because it allows you to see people you may not be able to on a regular basis while you talk to them. The communication is there: the visual and the verbal. It makes a difference.

CHAPTER 4

BOYZ N DA HOOD

"You could still be called daddy if the mother's not your wife"[4]

A stereotype is an oversimplified standardized image of a person or group, is damaging and often fueled through ignorance and miscommunication.

There were urban films in the early 1990s that were beginning to balance out the image of young Black fathers, showing these men in a more sympathetic light. The July 1991 release of *Boyz N' Da Hood* (Directed by John Singleton; 1991) highlighted a young Black father named Jason "Furious" Styles who was willing to take on the responsibility of fatherhood by taking in his young son Tre who was dropped off to him by Tre's mother Reva Devereaux, played by actress Angela Bassett, so he could learn how to be a man.

---

[4] Ed O.G. & Da Bulldogs, Be A Father To Your Child, 1991 – see appendix i.

That this film is still culturally relevant more than 20 years after its initial release is a testament to how powerful the message is. Showing the images of the inner city of South Central Los Angeles, California to a global audience, the movie is a coming of age story loosely based on the neighborhood where Singleton grew up. Similar to the intent of early "gangsta rap", Singleton used his talent to comment on the conditions of the ghettos in his hometown.

This film is revered more by some for the graphic violence and negativity it perpetuated on-screen than the dynamic father-son bond that clearly dominated the plot of the movie. I know this from my own personal viewing experience. The scenes that stuck in my mind were that of Ricky getting shot by rival gangbangers, and Doughboy exacting bloody revenge on the killers. It is no coincidence that these two scenes were the most violent in the film, but no less powerful in the context of the story.

Sometimes you have to give the people what they want to see or hear to get what you want them to see and hear across. Singleton showed how impoverished youth without a strong father figure in their life can get easily caught up in illegal activity through peer pressure or just the idea of being a part of a family of some kind.

The kid with the strict father uses protection when he has sex, puts the gun down when raw emotions say otherwise, and gets out of the car headed to pull a drive-by shooting, while the kids without the paternal figure becomes a teen father (Ricky), gets arrested at a young age (Doughboy), or gets shot and is bound to a wheelchair for the rest of his life (Chris). Pretty cut and dry.

Critically acclaimed actor Laurence Fishburne plays Furious while Academy Award nominee Cuba Gooding, Jr. plays his son Tre. Tre and his childhood friends grew up amidst poverty, violence, and drugs, an unfortunate reality that Tre became accustomed to from the time he and his friends stumble upon a rotting corpse, until the time he grows into a teenager.

Furious is instrumental in keeping Tre from straying down the wrong path, teaching him life lessons ranging from responsibility (raking the lawn and doing household chores), dealing with criminals (Furious fires after a burglar who breaks into the house, but tells Tre killing someone is not the right thing to do), corrupt cops, teen pregnancy, and fatherhood: "any fool with a dick can make a baby, but only a real man can raise his children."(*Boyz N' Da Hood*; Singleton, 1991*)*

Furious - whose steely resolve, stern voice and no-nonsense attitude justify his moniker - is the only father figure in the movie (Tre's friends brothers Ricky and Darrin "Doughboy" Baker live with their single mother) and a strong example of how a young Black father teaches his son right from wrong in dubious situations. He even takes on the responsibility of trying to educate Tre's friends.

One poignant example of Furious' dedication to his effort of being a good father to Tre is during his son's most emotional moment.

Ricky (played by actor Morris Chestnut), Tre's best friend and a young father on his way to college, gets shot and killed right in front of him by a rival gang. Tre is shattered by the tragedy and decides to avenge his friend's murder. Furious first talks Tre out of seeking revenge with the same gun he shot after the burglar with, but when Doughboy (played by rapper Ice Cube) and two of his friends drive up to go looking for the shooter, Tre secretly leaves with them.

Throughout the film, Furious uses a set of silver balls he rotates in his hands when he is stressed out. Worried that his son would be a victim of the endless cycle of retaliatory attacks prevalent in gangs, Furious rapidly works the stress balls around his fingers in a circular motion, the sound growing louder and louder.

A cut away to Tre in the back seat of the car shows his conflicting emotions about what he is about to do. When Tre asks and is ultimately let out of the car, Furious stops rotating the stress balls showing the impact of the father-son connection built throughout the film.

The sound of the stress balls is enhanced to give the effect that it caused Tre to get out of the car, but it is the foundation laid by Furious which allows Tre to use common sense to make a smart choice.

Although *Boyz N' Da Hood* depicts various scenes of negativity in the urban community (men degrading women, gang violence, and police corruption), one constant was the devotion of Furious to his son, a determination to instill values that would keep his son away from harm. Where Tre continuously caused problems as a child while living with his mother, he stayed out of trouble (fishing with his dad while Doughboy was stealing, refusing to drink a 40 oz. of beer that is passed to him) proving a young Black man can rise above his conditions and teach his child to do the same.

Ricky was a devoted teenage father and star football player. He made the decision to study for his Scholastic Aptitude Test (SAT) so he could get into college and earn a football scholarship for the sake of the betterment of his family.

There are scenes where he is studying to take his SAT and taking care of his young child. Unfortunately his last scene is as a bloodied corpse on his mother's couch in front of his girlfriend and infant. Ricky sadly became a casualty of his environment, a disturbing yet unfortunately common scene in urban neighborhoods.

The aforementioned rapper Ice Cube made his feature film debut in *Boyz N' Da Hood* as the tough older half brother of Rick starved for attention from his mother. With no father figure present, Cube's character embodied the stereotypical outcome of a fatherless child: shuffling in and out of jail at a young age, drinking alcohol, smoking and carrying a gun. At that time, Ice Cube had just left the rap group N.W.A. and it was thought that he was basically playing himself in the role.

Without N.W.A.'s reporting on the culture of urban neighborhoods in California, *Boyz N Da Hood* does not happen. N.W.A. brought national attention to Hip Hop music when it was basically written off as a fad. Unfortunately the music as a whole has been criticized and stereotyped by the media because of the hardcore subgenre in a way not dissimilar to how the young Black father is viewed. In many cases fatherhood in the Black community and Hip Hop are related and *Boyz* is a shining example.

The darker, less radio friendly fare that was "gangsta rap" came under constant attack, however the subject matter dealt with what the impoverished community was experiencing: homes with no fathers, drug abuse, gang violence, teen pregnancy, etc.

Ironically, the artists who were at the center of the stereotypical assertions about Hip Hop became devoted young fathers. Artists like *Snoop Doggy Dogg* (ne Calvin Broadus) have come under attack by political mouthpieces such as FOX News pundit Bill O'Reilly for the content of his music.

Politicians like the late Congresswoman C. Delores Tucker, and religious leader Dr. Calvin Butts attacked the message of "gangsta rap" by way of public speeches to Congress and organized protests where hundreds of "gangsta rap" compact discs were dumped on the street and stomped on.

I remember seeing highlights, or lowlights, of the "gangsta rap" CD demolition on the evening news. I always felt that the crowd of parishioners, politicians, citizens, and parents were taking the wrong approach.

The demonstration was supposed to speak out against music that was misogynistic and violent, yet the demonstration in itself was a violent act. Here are these people crushing a few hundred CD's with their feet and a bulldozer, dancing on the images of these "violent" rappers to make a point, yet the artists are selling a few million copies. They could care less about protests from a monetary standpoint, but stomping on their likeness would only serve to irritate and aggravate the artists prompting them to record music that was more defiantly profane in a direct response to the protesters further widening the chasm of misunderstanding between the two parties.

Evidence of this division can be found in the battle between *Tupac Shakur* and Tucker. Shakur repeatedly mentioned the Congresswoman in his songs, most notably in his hit song *"How Do You Want It"*[5]. Tucker later claimed that Tupac's repeated verbal attacks on her ruined her love/sex life.

Hip Hop music has thrived on resistance. The lyrics speak on resistance to the ills of the rappers' environment and rebellious youth. If you're stomping on these CD's on television, it's like

---

[5] In the song from the first disc of his double CD "All Eyes On Me", Tupac raps "(C.) Delores Tucker ain't a friend to me/ instead of trying to help a brother try to take his G's" (Note: The unedited version says something different – see appendix).

telling kids they can't have something, which is going to make them gravitate toward it even more.

The television, radio and print media has played a big role in perpetuating these negative images of Black on Black crime and misogyny on wax. If that is all a young person sees, where is the hope for something better, especially if the family structure is fractured?

****

N.W.A. an acronym for *"Niggaz Wit Attitude"* was a group of young men from the mean streets of Compton California who hit the rap scene hard in 1988 with their second album *Straight Outta Compton* (follow-up to 1987's *NWA and the Posse*) rife with foul language and imagery exposing crime, poverty, and police brutality in their inner city surroundings. Being one of the first groups to brandish guns in rap videos, N.W.A. was banned from many mainstream U.S. radio stations and video shows. The group consisted of Eazy E, Dr. Dre, MC Ren, DJ Yella, The D.O.C and Ice Cube.

It was N.W.A. who called their music "reality rap" drawing the ire of the Los Angeles Police Department with the seminal *"Fu-- Tha Police"*, an indictment of the police department so scathing it prompted the FBI to write a "cease and desist" letter to the group's record label Ruthless Records. Even though the group parted ways over financial disputes, N.W.A. epitomized the anger and disenfranchisement of urban youth at the time.

According to a feature story on the group in the June 2011 issue of *Ebony* magazine, former group member MC Ren stated that it was in fact a reporter, morbidly afraid of the group during a live interview, who went on to coin their music as "gangsta rap" in a subsequent news story to the disgust of the crew.

Ice Cube was a lead writer of the group during their controversial heyday. Although he was very gifted in crafting hardcore lyrics that spoke to the people of his neighborhood, Cube himself grew up with his father. Cube credits his father for teaching him how to be a man.

It was perhaps being around a stable family that has allowed Cube to maintain the relationship with his own wife for more than 20 years without any public rumors or stories of infidelity in an industry filled with opportunists.

Cube, a father of four children, credited the support of his future wife in guiding him to make the tough decision to leave N.W.A. amidst allegations of financial impropriety. Cube took a huge risk starting his career from scratch as a solo artist, especially with his first born only a few months old.

The gamble paid off with one of the classic albums in all of Hip Hop: *Amerikkka's Most Wanted*. From there Ice Cube has become one of the most acclaimed writer/actor/directors in Hollywood recently producing a successful string of family comedies *Are We There Yet?,* and *Are We Done Yet?*

Once controversial, only because he felt a duty to use his music to speak on Black issues others wanted to sweep under the rug, Cube has grown into a devoted family man who focuses his energy into providing for his wife and kids by improving his image to where he can expand his role and be accepted as a major player in the White-dominated film industry.

Cube is still performing and making music today. Whenever he performs nowadays he is usually joined on stage by his two older sons *OMG* and *Doughboy* (named after his father's *Boyz N Da Hood* character) rocking crowds to some of their father's old hits and as featured artists on his new songs. Like Reverend Run (formerly DJ Run of the legendary Run-DMC), Cube has passed the torch to his sons (Rev Run's kids Jo-Jo and Diggy rhyme just like their dad[6]) and continues his musical legacy in the process. *OMG* (ne O'Shea Jackson, Jr.) played the role of his dad in the critically acclaimed *N.W.A.* biopic *"Straight Outta Compton"* released in the summer of 2015.

One may ask why Cube is so well-received now as opposed to his days as a "gangsta" rapper? I believe it is because an entirely new generation of people have no idea who the group *N.W.A* was. That

---

[6] Both sets of fathers and sons shared a freestyle segment during the 2010 BET Hip Hop Awards.

period of Cube's life began over 25 years ago, before the majority of social media savvy kids and teens were born.

A lot of today's generation is all about the present and don't have the patience to learn the history of the music they listen to. This is why today's rappers can remake another artist's song from 15 years ago and most kids will believe it is an original recording. The rapper may call it paying homage, but it is not paying homage unless the audience knows who made the original.

That being said, I am happy that artists like Ice Cube have come to a place where they are no longer defined by their controversial beginnings. It is a testament to his longevity in the business. He did not fade away like most artists of that era, but demonstrated his business acumen and versatility beginning with the cult classic *"Friday"* in 1995 which he wrote and directed. Showing people that you are more than what they expect you to be always earns respect.

While it can be said that Cube toned down his image in the interest of making money and being able to expand his brand, becoming a father has equally life-altering effects. In the best interest of the child, young fathers may instinctively cut down on swearing (comedian Eddie Murphy has stated his children are the reason he has done this), drinking, and staying out late at night in an effort to set a better example.

It is important to remember these artists rap about their environment more often than not and poverty, drugs, crooked cops, and gangs was what they saw around them. They are telling the stories of young men and women who can't speak for themselves. If the critics and powers that be really wanted to put an end to "gangsta rap", stop giving these kids something negative to write and subsequently rap about by putting an end to the economic disparity between the ghetto and suburbia.

CHAPTER 5

MENACE II SOCIETY

Menace II Society (*New Line Cinema directed by twin brothers Allen and Albert Hughes, 1993*) is one of my favorite movies because it was a learning experience for me. It validated what *Boyz N' Da Hood* started: giving me insight into the West Coast, a world apart from Brooklyn.

The film is well-known for glorifying Black urban lifestyle in the low income neighborhoods of California bringing the drug use, violence, misogyny, drug dealing, car theft, and lack of parental guidance voiced in "gangsta rap" records to a larger audience. *Menace* along with the aforementioned *Boyz N' Da Hood* spawned numerous copycat films depicting urban life on the West Coast giving birth to the derogatory term "'hood flick".

The companies releasing the movies, Columbia and New Line Cinema for *Boyz* and *Menace* respectively, had just as much a financial stake in the success of these films as Singleton and The

Hughes Brothers. Films like *New Jack City* (*directed by Mario Van Peebles, 1991*) and *Juice* (*directed by Ernest R. Dickerson, 1992*), were New York's version of life in the ghettos of the Big Apple. These were films that were just as violent, but criticized far less than their West Coast counterparts due to the fact that the West Coast urban lifestyle was more notorious.

Helicopters rarely flew over the streets of New York unless it was tourists who paid to take the trip over Manhattan. In the 'hoods of Los Angeles it was a regular occurrence. Not to mention the gang culture, a staple of California that would ultimately be co-opted on the East Coast.

Both films are important because it exposed the conditions that urban youth have to deal with in underprivileged neighborhoods, but unlike *Boyz*, the main character in *Menace* is forced to raise himself.

In *Menace* actor Samuel L. Jackson played Tat, the father of the main character Caine (played by newcomer Tyrin Turner) in the opening flashback scene of the movie. Where Furious was determined to make sure his son did not become a victim of his surroundings, Tat embodies the image of the stereotypical Black father as verbally abusive, violent, irresponsible, and immature.

Although Tat lived in the house with Caine, a little boy in the opening scene, his inattentiveness and total disregard for his son set the stage for the destructive direction of Caine's life throughout the rest of the film. Tat is positioned at a card table with his "friends",

54

while an older Caine describes the scene in the house using a voiceover.

Tat, immersed in his card game, does not notice his son walking through the house at an hour when he should be in bed. Caine's mother, strung out on drugs, is incoherent while looking for a hit.

The house is full of people smoking, and consuming alcohol, not a nurturing environment for a young child. Caine finds solace outside the house with a young man named Pernell. Pernell, a teenager, is not a great influence as he gives Caine a sip of liquor and teaches him how to hold a gun when Caine inquires about it.

After Tat kills one of his "friends" during a disagreement at the card table he finally notices his son, who witnessed the murder.

Tat is never heard from again in the movie, just a voiceover from Caine informing viewers that Tat was shot to death years later.

The images in the opening sequence of *Menace* show a one-sided view of the father-son relationship that led to a life of gratuitous violence, crime and drug dealing for Caine. As he gets older the cycle is repeated with Caine teaching another little boy - ironically Pernell's son - how to hold a gun while playing video games.

While this might be a reality to some young Black fathers and children at the time, it is not a realistic portrayal of all young Black fathers. There are Black fathers who do not endanger the lives of their children by giving them a gun or alcohol to drink.

Still *Menace II Society* was a movie that was canonized as a classic in urban communities. The influence and popularity of the film, with countless rappers referencing portions of the movie in their lyrics for the next decade, set a dangerous precedent feeding the stereotype of the role of the young Black father and the young Black man as a violent criminal.

The film was further criticized as life imitated art. Numerous reports of violence in the movie theaters where *Menace* was being screened dominated the news.

Unfortunately many young people can relate to the negative imagery depicted in the film which is precisely why the film was so successful, however despite all the violence, which was true to the story, the message in the film centered around the evolution of Caine. The irony here is that Caine admitted that Pernell was someone he idolized as more of a father figure during a tearful jailhouse visit.

Pernell, although locked up, gives Caine some sage "fatherly" advice. He tells Caine not to be like him, that the way he was leading his life was not cool. He tells Caine to look after his son and show him a positive way of life. In other words break the cycle.

Caine takes these words to heart as he indeed protects Pernell's boy from danger at the end of the movie. After initially fleeing the bullets being sprayed in a vengeful drive-by shooting, Caine returns to save Pernell's son, who is in the crossfire, taking multiple bullets to the chest. Once the shooting ends, Caine is shown covering the boy with his body. Once the boy is safe, Caine dies. The scene shows Caine has paternal instincts his father Tat never possessed.

Menace II Society is a strong film based on the harsh realities of life for underprivileged youth. Unfortunately there are people in the world like O-Dog, Caine and A-Wax. Why were these kids a "menace to society"? Because they were young, Black and didn't give a damn if they lived or died. What positive options did they have?

Who made the young Black man the definition of a menace to society? Why wasn't *Son of Sam, Jeffrey Dahmer, David Koresh* or the men that assassinated *John F. Kennedy, Martin Luther King, Jr.* and *John Lennon* a menace to society? What about the kids that orchestrated the mass murders at Columbine, Virginia Tech, and Arizona? The lunatic that shot up Sandy Hook elementary school killing 20 harmless first graders? Is it because they took their own lives as well that they are not branded? They are not menaces because they are not physically present to be branded as such? They were all cowards! The guy that nearly took Gabrielle Giffords' life in Arizona was said to be mentally unstable. The punk that massacred moviegoers watching *"The Dark Knight"* in Colorado tried to use an insanity defense, appearing in court wide eyed with pink hair.

The bullied White kid that finally snapped and committed murder was a common theme in the suburbs of middle America and there was never a stigma or label attached. It was always "what went wrong?" It's the same thing that's wrong with our Black youth: lack of guidance, lack of conversation.

Yet Black people don't have that luxury of introspection. We are always angry. Like there is nothing to be angry about. Check our history and forgive us for not smiling all the time.

There was a point where I started calling my mother to wish her Happy Father's Day because she really played both roles as best as she could. My mother instilled in me the importance of being a leader and not a follower. She also did her best to raise me with all the comforts a middle-class income could afford.

Never once did I watch *Menace* and say I am going to go out and carjack someone or hold up a liquor store. Who knows, maybe if my mother struggled to make ends meet after my father left and we lived off food stamps in a housing project my anger at my living conditions may have gotten the better of me, or maybe not. There is a point where you can't keep using your living conditions as an excuse not to succeed, but the adult has to have the same never say die attitude or the child won't believe it.

There were times in my life where my finances were not the best and bills were due and things got tight, but I never looked to do anything illegal nor took any shortcuts to improve my situation. All I had was a faith in God that He would make a way for me and my family. Sometimes it's as simple as praying. You have to be patient because the blessing won't come when you want it or expect it, but it comes right on time. These are lessons I learned as a youth that children today are not hearing on a regular basis.

The characters in *Menace* did not have that foundation. We never saw *O-Dog's* parents and he was a minor (under 18 years of age) in the film. *Caine's* grandparents tried to instill some faith in him, but at his advanced age God was not in his belief system. From seeing gun violence from your father and your mother addicted to drugs, there was no one to show him what was right from wrong. It's hard to tell a young man who practically raised himself and survived in a dangerous environment what to do, but the effort still has to be there because ultimately "thugs" and "gangsters" are looking for love and acceptance they probably never received from family members.

What would have served a better purpose is if all the people that were complaining about the film and its potential affect on young children took a step back to see that those characters existed in real life, reached out to these impoverished communities and showed these children that there is an alternative to joining gangs and a life of crime.

Along with positive media images and movie characters, national and state governments have to take some responsibility to ensure that there is a proper distribution of funds to impoverished communities.

This could go a long way towards improving the gloomy images of trash on the streets, urine-soaked staircases in project buildings, liquor stores on almost every corner, and pot-hole littered streets.

The lack of job opportunities and negligence by city and state officials are just as culpable as the media outlets that report on, but do not provide a solution to, this troubling trend.

While it is plausible that Black males may encounter biases that keep them from being accepted to the best schools or attaining a decent job based on preconceived notions of others, the question has to be asked: is it always institutionalized racism or the result of being subject to or the victim of ignorant behavior by our young Black men that makes people assume the worst of every Black man they come in contact with?

It is the old what came first the chicken or the egg theory, yet this cannot be used as an excuse to accept being passed over for jobs or to fail. This is where these organizations, businesses, school boards, and government are vital. Teach these young men to respect and conduct themselves with dignity. Give these young men a viable option to the lure of the streets, a better familial environment to the one offered by gang members. Give these young Black men the confidence to show these gatekeepers the error of their assuming ways.

That is all.

CHAPTER 6

"PAPA'S GOT A BRAND NEW EXCUSE"

I remember seeing a less-than-positive characterization of a Black father on a television sitcom which had originally purported to present more positive images of Black families. *The Fresh Prince of Bel-Air*, aired on NBC between 1990 and 1996, starring rapper-turned-actor Will Smith. Smith plays Will, a high school student sent to live with his wealthy relatives in California by his mother because he was getting into too much trouble in his Philadelphia neighborhood (sound familiar?).

In this case Furious was Uncle Phil, a no-nonsense judge who's strict disciplinarian countenance was the perfect contrast to Will's antics.

Throughout the series there is no mention of Will's biological father. However, during one episode in 1994, aptly titled *"Papa's Got a Brand New Excuse"*, Will's biological father Lou, played by actor Ben Vereen, arrives at the doorstep of the Bel-Air home. Lou is the typical negative stereotype of the Black father in this episode, leaving his family when Will was five years old, instilling hope in his child by returning with promises of spending time together only to leave his child again.

Lou was met with skepticism by Will and his Uncle Phillip Banks at first, but while Uncle Phil holds firm on his doubts that Lou is ready to be a responsible father, Will slowly begins to gain hope that he would have the father he never saw growing up. In the scene where Will is speaking to his cousin Carlton, he beams:

"You know Carlton, up until a few days ago I never thought I'd see my father again. I never even think about it 'cuz I knew it was never gonna happen. But I still managed to keep the fantasy. Now it's real. I can't believe how lucky I am."

Throughout the first four years of the show, the relationship between uncle and nephew was filled with good-natured jokes that Phil was usually on the receiving end of. However, in this episode, the return of Lou really hit Phil hard.

After Will tells Phil that he doesn't care what his uncle thinks about his moving out of the house to spend time with Lou because Phil is not his father, Phil makes the case to his wife that he was Will's father for four years. Phil returns to see Will after the heated exchange and the two men apologize to each other. Phil reluctantly wishes Will luck with Lou and the impending summer trip.

Uncle Phil's role in Will's life is what has been called "social fatherhood". Michael Connor and Joseph White write in their article *Fatherhood In Contemporary Black America* (*Black Scholar,*

Summer 2007), "social fatherhood encompasses father figures, men who are not biological fathers but who provide a significant degree of nurturance, moral and ethical guidance, companionship, emotional support, and financial responsibility in the lives of children."

This idea is central to Phil's argument; that he is the only real father Will has known and the fact that Will is so quick to leave with a biological father who hasn't been a part of Will's life hurts him.

The episode ends with Lou's character deserting Will yet again, not even having the courage to tell Will in person that he is leaving. Phil scolds Lou:

"Will is not a coat that you hang in the closet then pick it up when you're ready to wear it…he's not supposed to be here for you, you're supposed to be here for him."

Lou cites a rough upbringing as a reason for leaving his family, but Phil refutes the excuse:

"I was there, but I didn't run out on my family. I was there every day for them because that's what a man does."

Will walks in the room just as Lou is walking out of the room, symbolic in that Lou's back is turned. Lou dances around the fact that he is leaving again, but Will catches on to the weak attempt by Lou at postponing their trip. With the feeling of detachment and anger returning to his face, Will simply addresses his father as

"Lou". Will's subsequent tirade summed up the feeling of most Black children abandoned by their fathers:

"Why should I be mad? At least he said goodbye this time… ain't like I'm still five years old, you know. Ain't like I'm sitting up every night asking my mom when's daddy coming home, you know. Who needs him? He wasn't there to teach me how to shoot my first basket, but I learned didn't I? Got pretty damn good at it didn't I, Uncle Phil? Got through my first date without him, right? I learned how to drive, learned how to shave, I learned how to fight without him, I had 14 great birthdays without him he never even sent me a damn card, TO HELL WITH HIM!"

After a pause Will continues "*I ain't need him then, don't need him now.*" Seconds later Will tearfully crumbles into Phil's arms asking why Lou doesn't want him.

This is a scene that is most likely all too familiar to children in the United States; however the segment serves to illustrate both the negative and positive role of the young Black father with Lou being the selfish father running away from his responsibilities, while Uncle Phil serves as the strong Black father and source of stability for Will.

I remember watching that episode and immediately noticing how different the tone of the show was. Before this Will was sort of a class clown. I tuned in to The Fresh Prince of Bel-Air on Monday nights expecting to laugh, however in this particular episode I saw

Will yell at Uncle Phil for the first time, an outburst that immediately made me sit up and pay extra attention.

I thought about the similarities in my own life. If my father, gone for five years at that point, showed up at my doorstep, how would I react? Would I say all is forgiven and risk another guilt trip from my mom or take out my anger on him?

I felt Will made the transition into an actor to be reckoned with in this episode. The sudden appearance of someone you hadn't seen in years will stir up a mix of emotions and Will touched on every one of them.

****

I have three women I affectionately called my "second" mother, but I never thought about a social father. If I had to name someone it would be my Uncle Barry. He was always an unceasing source of support for my mother. He was definitely someone my sister and I could count on. His sense of humor and quiet leadership during our family outings made him someone I always wanted to be around.

He wasn't my primary caretaker like Uncle Phil was to Will, but he was definitely someone I felt confident talking to. He was very instrumental in helping my mother get her current home, he gave an emotional speech at our wedding, and he has been very supportive of my writing.

CHAPTER 7

RECKLESS ABANDON

I was born in 1978. Anyone born in the mid to late seventies will tell you that the 1980s was the best decade. In the '80s life was simple. The only source of stress or aggravation at the time was going to school, not so much school itself, but homework and book reports.

I actually liked grade school. My teachers were cool for the most part, and I was very athletic so I made a lot of friends playing schoolyard games like Fly's Up, Tag, Freeze Tag, Suicide (a game where you threw either a tennis ball or blue handball against the wall and if you dared to catch the ball and dropped it, you had to run to the wall and avoid getting spiked, dodge ball style, with the ball from whoever grabbed it), punch ball, and 1-2-3 hold football before school started and during lunchtime.

I was able to listen to a great variety of music and see the accompanying videos on shows like Friday Night Videos and New York Hot Tracks of artists like Michael Jackson (R.I.P), Madonna,

Prince, Wham (a group that featured a young George Michael), The Cars, The Police, Huey Lewis, etc.

Hip Hop music was fresh on the scene and the '80s ushered in instant classics like "La Di Da Di" performed by Slick Rick and Doug E. Fresh, "Sucker MC's", "Rock Box", and "Walk This Way" performed by Run-DMC, "South Bronx" performed by KRS-One, "Ain't No Half Steppin'" performed by Big Daddy Kane, "The Freaks Come Out at Night" and "One Love" performed by Whodini, and so on.

Who could forget about the cartoons: The Real Ghostbusters, Duck Tales, Muppet Babies, Fat Albert & the Cosby Kids (already in syndication from the '70s), Alvin & the Chipmunks, Smurfs, the New Archies, rap group Kid N' Play had their own cartoon, WWF (now WWE) Wrestling had their own "Superstars of Wrestling" cartoon featuring wrestlers from the wildly popular weekly shows that included Saturday Night's Main Event (you know you were glued to your seat when this came on at 11:30 p.m.). If you got into problems with someone more likely than not it would be settled with fisticuffs, not weapons.

The fondest memories I have about the '80s was that my family was together. My mom and my aunt would alternate which house would host Thanksgiving and Christmas dinner respectively, a tradition that was as highly anticipated as revelers from all over the world waiting for hours in freezing temperatures in Times Square for the ball to drop to usher in a new year.

It seemed like every Saturday night there was a house party in the basement of our two-story house on 32nd Street between Snyder and Tilden in Brooklyn. I spent the majority of my pre-teen years on that block in the number 98 house. My mother, father, sister and I rented the 2nd floor of the house. The second floor had a patio and from there I could see onto the streets below, which was only depressing when I couldn't go outside and I watched my friends play.

I remember taking naps during the evening and waking up to get dressed for the festivities. Who needed the club? The landlord and his family were of Jamaican descent and he had a boatload of records. I was treated to the finest in reggae and dancehall music from artists like Gregory Issacs, Supercat, Pinchers, Courtney Melody, Admiral Bailey and more. Even today I maintain a great appreciation for the classic dancehall music of my youth.

There was the "Big 4" birthday party thrown for my uncle, my godmother's husband, my next door neighbor, and I as we all shared a birthday in the first week of September. I was honored to be celebrated with these three adults as I was all of four years old.

There were parties in the Baldwin section of Long Island thrown by my paternal grandmother's brother. It was nothing to take the trip to Long Island from Brooklyn when a house party was taking place; this is how good the parties were. I was too young to fully appreciate it, but I remember the same classic reggae and calypso music being played and, more importantly, the pool in the backyard.

This was a main attraction for me every time I came to this house. It was during one of those famous parties where I almost killed myself playing around the pool, but that is a story for another book.

My earliest memories of my dad were good ones. He was very much into sports and cartoons, which at the time I thought was weird, but now I can understand how adults can get caught up.

An electrician by trade, I occasionally accompanied my dad to his job in Queens. A simple sign that read "AXEL Electronics" greeted us as we rode in a gray Mercury car.

The gray Mercury, a two door sports car that looked similar to the Delorean from the *Back to the Future* movies, would be burned into my memory for the wrong reason soon enough, but for now it was the family vehicle. Not only did it get us from point A to B, but me to McDonalds on Thursday evenings.

This became a tasty weekly tradition - possibly because Thursday was payday for my dad - I looked forward to. I would order my Happy Meal or Cheeseburger meal while my sister would go with a Big Mac or McDLT, a specialty sandwich that was out at the time. After a while I became curious, and envious, of my sister's weekly order of two-story sandwiches. So I did what any kid would, I showed that I was a big kid by forgoing my small cheeseburger and ordered a Big Mac.

The science to eating a Big Mac is to hold the burger tight so the patties, lettuce, and special sauce won't shift and spill out of the bottom when you bite into it. It took me years to figure this out (I actually celebrated the first time I ate a Big Mac cleanly), and during my first attempt, the sandwich proved way too big for my ambitious taste buds.

After two bites, I lost the middle roll of bread that separates the two patties. This keeps the structure of the Big Mac together, so it was downhill from there. I finished the top sesame seed bun before the meat and it was a reclamation project just to save face.

I eventually threw away half the sandwich, a messy glob of special sauce, onions, lettuce and half-eaten meat. I took solace in that I kept the mess inside the box saving the Mercury from any residue. Needless to say next week it was back to my cheeseburger. I might have ordered Chicken McNuggets as I did not want to see another burger so soon after the Big Mac debacle.

Going to McDonalds is a request I fulfill for Trey whenever he asks. He knows when I roll up to the drive thru window that he is getting his "4-piece nuggets happy meal for a boy." I don't have a specific day set up for these trips to the golden arches, but the symbolism is not lost on me. Sometimes I will take him inside, sit down to eat and just look at him.

On Saturdays I would get up at 6 a.m. to watch cartoons, unless it was bowling season. My dad was in a bowling league at Van Wyck

Lanes in Queens located directly across the street from his job at Axel Electronics. Every Wednesday night after work he participated in his league as a member of a three-man team. I believe his average was 180, pretty good for a bowler. I would see his gray and white-striped bowling bag around the house, custom bowling shoes and bowling glove and knew I wanted to bowl too.

Bowling looked easy enough to me. Just keep the ball from going into the gutter on each side, and knock down all the pins in two attempts, preferably one. I didn't take into account the oil-slicked lane's affect on the trajectory of the ball, the fact that the pins were set at an angle where the ball had to hit the head (or lead) pin at a certain spot to initiate a chain reaction that would cause all the pins to fall. I just knew it looked like fun.

I had the honor of watching my dad in action one Wednesday night. The focus and concentration in his eyes as he held his bowling ball out in front of him let me know how serious he took the sport. I thought it was cool how he put just enough spin on the ball, as it slid down the lane close to the right gutter, that it turned right into the head pin about ten feet from the pins. I would later inject my own curveball into my game, the first of many delivery methods I would experiment with. I joined a children's league at the same bowling alley shortly thereafter. I can't remember what the full name of the league was, but I know the acronym was YABA.

Just like track and field, bowling had divisions of sub-bantam and bantam. I started at the sub-bantam level and used the league to get my fundamentals down. My dad taught me to aim for the second arrow on the right side of the lane since I was a right-handed bowler. Aiming for a bunch of arrows sounds easy enough, but doing it consistently is the key.

This is why, like golf, professional bowlers need extreme quiet before they deliver the ball. I always wondered as a kid watching the Professional Bowlers Association (PBA) Tour (a mandatory program for any bowling fanatic) why you could hear a pin drop while the bowler is staring at the lanes, but as soon as the ball hits the pine it is like a switch is flipped triggering crowd noise as the ball spins toward the pins and riotous applause when the bowler gets a strike.

Hand/eye coordination is very important in bowling, along with the ability to block out distractions. One small flick of the wrist can be the difference between a strike, a 7-10 split (where one pin from each end of the lane remain standing), and a gutter ball.

I picked up on bowling terminology quickly. I learned that a turkey was three strikes in a row, each pin on the lane is numbered relative to their position (see the aforementioned 7-10 split reference), and, in New York anyway, the left side of the headpin facing the bowler is the Brooklyn side while the right side of the head pin is the

Queens side, and you always want your bowling ball to hit the headpin on the Queens side for maximum effect.

For all the bowling terminology I picked up, I couldn't keep score for the life of me. At first I could care less because I just wanted to learn how to bowl, but as I got better and started to care about my average, I made it my business to learn (the final straw was during one of my 5th grade bowling trips to Gil Hodges Lanes, the automatic scoring machine broke down and we had to score manually, although I was the best bowler in the class I could not keep score). I made sure I learned quickly after that.

I was not a die-hard bowler as of yet so I did not have a need to get my own bowling ball. I was perfectly content with using the bowling alley house balls. As long as the holes in the bowling ball fit my fingers properly I went to work. As I advanced in skill level, it became mandatory that I get my own ball.

Owning your bowling ball is a sign of professionalism. If you weren't that good having your own ball made you look the part and scared the competition, until it was time to bowl and your lack of skill was exposed.

The selection of a bowling ball is arguably the equivalent of choosing an outfit. The brand of the bowling ball was important; an elite brand at the time was *Ebonite*, for example. The color and texture of the ball was important, although I am not sure why but for me it was for vanity purposes. The final component to a professional looking bowling ball is the inscription of the bowler's name on it. If someone saw your name on your ball he knew you meant business.

Once I became comfortable at the bowling alley, I began traveling to my league games on my own via city bus. Van Wyck Lanes had arcade games; one I particularly grew fond of was a game called Shinobi. This was the era of the original Sega as Nintendo was creeping on the horizon and I had a bunch of sports games, but I was still open to play adventure games.

I arrived at the bowling alley usually a few minutes before my match started every week and I would always see a huge crowd in front of this Shinobi game. One Saturday after my league games were finished (I believe my team lost the series), I noticed Shinobi was available. I put in a quarter and started to play. I was immediately hooked to the star-throwing, sword-wielding ninja. It was only a matter of time until I started coming to the alley up to two hours early to master the game.

My dad used to watch the broadcast of the Professional Bowlers Tour on Saturday afternoons, so that became as much a part of my Saturday as the morning cartoons. It was my routine to bowl my league games then come home in time to watch the professionals on ABC.

Guys like Marshall Holman, Brian Voss, Pete Weber, Amletto Monacelli, and Norm Duke were weekly fixtures on ABC as they consistently bowled the highest average for that week to make it on live television. These were the people I wanted to emulate if I was going to be a better bowler. At the time I had no intention of being a professional bowler, I just wanted to do what my dad was doing. There are times I will stop and watch the PBA Tour on ESPN nowadays and see the bowlers I grew up watching still finishing top 5 for the week in contention for another championship. Good memories.

I did want to play Little League baseball, which is something my dad did not do. I watched a lot of New York Mets baseball in the '80s and wanted to be Darryl Strawberry. My dad attempted to teach me how to play soccer during our trips to Prospect Park, but I would always see a group of kids in bright orange uniforms practicing.

These kids intrigued me with their orange trucker hat-style baseball caps with the black "B" on the front. Their uniform shirt read *"Bonnies"*. I wanted to play for the *Bonnies* and asked my dad to find out how to join from the coach. One kid I went to elementary school with named Lamarr was a member of the team; that made me want to be on the team even more.

I never made the *Bonnies*. I am not sure what the issue was, maybe the cost to join was too much, but I was disappointed I wouldn't get to play Little League baseball at that moment.

****

In the spring of 1988 I was in the fourth grade at Public School 235 in Brooklyn New York. I was in the final couple of months of a good grade school career in the Soar Program. I already missed the deadline to take the exam for early entry into Phillippa Schuyler Middle School so I would be starting fifth grade at the P.S. 235 Annex.

Changes in my scholastic home would mirror changes in my own residence. I started to notice strange behavior in my dad. He was coming home later than usual which caused a lot of arguments with my mother. The bickering was something I was not used to, though I believe my parents fought as married couples do, never when I was around. I knew the arguments were serious because it would wake me out of my sleep.

My parents put any differences they had aside to attend my graduation from P.S. 235. When I started fifth grade at the annex, I was displaced after a few weeks when my teacher left the school. The class was disintegrated and the students were split up between the other classes. I was lucky enough to be sent to a class higher than the one I was in. Not only did I have to get acclimated to a new class, new teacher, and new students, the conflict between my parents continued to escalate.

I began to act out in school; talking in class during the lesson, and falling out of my chair on purpose to get a laugh. At the time I thought I was being a class clown. Problem was I had never been a class clown before. I usually laughed at other jokers in the class who took off their shoes or made weird noises to distract the students, but

I never took part in the shenanigans (save for flying a paper airplane or two).

My grades eventually started to slip, but the weird thing is I didn't physically try to stop doing my school work. I was definitely distracted, but underestimated the effect my parent's arguing had on my ability to excel in the classroom.

One night I was awakened out of my sleep to my mother yelling. My dad had come home late one too many times and my mother was not having it. I had never seen my mother so angry unless she was coming after me. They were in the kitchen as the steps that led down to the front door began where the kitchen ended. I guess my mother heard my dad coming up the steps and met him. I had walked from my room into the hallway adjacent from the bathroom which was only a few feet away from where my parents were standing.

What were they arguing about? What could be so bad that they did not even realize I was standing there? That particular argument ended so terribly I feared for the safety of my parents. I no longer wanted to go to school because I did not want to come home and find that one of them was seriously injured or worse.

The morning after I witnessed that nasty fight, I noticed my dad sitting on the floor in the living room watching television. I walked up to him and sat down. He was calm, laughing at the show that was on television. It was like nothing happened. I didn't know what to think about his nonchalant attitude. Then I remembered they did not even know I was standing within inches of them during their spat.

I know I wasn't dreaming about the events that took place the night before. My dad was trying to play it cool as was his normal demeanor. Still the events of the past few weeks was far from normal. I was not used to displays of violence, physical or otherwise, and I was scared; scared for the future of our family. I couldn't sit quiet.

"Dad-Neville."

I softly uttered my nickname for my dad, a combination of his parental title and his first name. Once I got his attention, I asked a question along the lines of was he going to leave my mother, the thought of such a thing happening tore me up inside. Tears began to roll down both of my cheeks. My dad was reassuring, calmly embracing me as he told me he was not going to leave. That was the end of the conversation. Even though I was still scared I also felt a sense of relief at my dad's answer. I believed what he told me. Why would he lie?

A few days later while lying in bed I heard the constant sound of footsteps back and forth throughout the house. My mom was at work so it was only my dad, my older sister and I in the house. My sister was still sleeping next to me so it had to be my dad walking around.

I decided to get up and see what all the activity was. I got up just in time to see my dad going out the door and down the stairs toward the front door. He was unaware that I saw him leave. Curious I walked through the living room area to a door leading to the patio.

I looked over the railing to see my dad throw a traveling bag in the trunk of the gray Mercury which was idling in the driveway. There wasn't anything suspicious about his actions. There was no looking around or behind him. There was no indication that this would be the last time I would see him until I was in my mid-twenties.

With a right turn out of the driveway he was gone leaving a trail of smoke out the exhaust of the gray Mercury.

Just like that.

No goodbye. Not a word. I am not sure if he knew that would be his last time at that house. There is no way he would just leave like that right?

****

My father went through great lengths to avoid taking care of me. To hear this from my mother I knew it was from, for lack of a better term, a biased source. My mother had been hurt very deeply by my father's deception and she made sure I knew what a lowlife he was to her.

One evening the phone rang. I answered to hear my father on the other line. I hadn't seen him in a couple of days yet he spoke to me like everything was normal. He promised me McDonalds that coming Thursday night. Well, good because I had looked forward to my weekly Mickey D's like Friday at three o'clock (which meant school was out until Monday), and I didn't want to give that up. After that conversation he never showed up. I didn't get McDonalds that Thursday. What I did get was a tongue-lashing from my mother for even engaging in conversation with him.

My mom's pain was still fresh and she felt any communication with my father was a betrayal to her. I obviously didn't understand the magnitude of what was happening. I still thought my father was coming home and the phone call gave me hope.

'Maybe he just took a mini-vacation.'

'Maybe he had a job interview… in another state,' I thought.

Losing his job was one of many transgressions that was the beginning of the end so to speak. There were no cell phones so once my mother changed the phone number to our house all communication was lost. I knew then he wasn't coming back.

I never cried again for my father like I did that day I approached him about if he was leaving my mother. I guess subconsciously I felt betrayed. I was vulnerable at that moment and he lied to my face. He had a plan. There is always a plan. You don't make a life-altering decision like walking away from your marriage and family on a whim. If he was forced out why not say something?

I felt like one of those little kids on soap operas that always get sent out of the room whenever the adults want to talk about something. I had only lived a decade at the time, but I was not stupid. Kids always know when something is wrong, even at two years old. Children absorb everything and they will eventually let it out whether it is later that day, that month, or, worse yet, years down the road when they are adults in their own relationship.

I figured out something was not right before my father abandoned us and I think I deserved an explanation. For that reason, I was angry. That deception at my most emotional point is probably a reason I struggle with showing emotion to this day.

I didn't understand separation. I never had to experience it. I began to think that my father didn't really care about my well-being. Sure he would stop by his sister's house and ask about me, but there were hurtful allegations that he cleaned out all the money from a joint account shared with my mother, and either refused to work or worked off the books so he wouldn't have to pay child support.

My mother recently revealed to me that my father told her that he was down South working on getting a new job. She said he promised her when he got some money he would come back home and pay the rent. She also told me my father told her that he knows she could raise my sister and I. He essentially told her that she didn't need him there because she was doing a bang up job already. She could handle two kids and the responsibility of keeping a roof over our heads on her own.

If I knew the term "deadbeat" at that time, a picture of my father would be in the dictionary right next to the word with his thumbs up.

He lived a borough away in Queens (with another woman who my mother confronted in court), but for years no one knew where. Combine that with what my mother was telling me, I almost felt - check that, I did feel guilty for even talking to my father on the phone.

I never met the man my mother was describing. My father never beat me, rarely yelled at me. I was not savvy (read: old) enough to command a better explanation from her so I could form an opinion. Maybe he was evil.

I felt so bad I tried to physically hurt myself. I thought it was wrong for me to try to reach out to my father. I was forced to take sides. I wondered if the woman he was living with had kids of her own. Was he taking care of other children while I was alone? My sister would leave in the fall of 1989 to start college at Delaware State University so it would just be me and my mother.

I became increasingly angry and resentful. I thought I had to be. I ripped up pictures of my father, even burned a photo while proclaiming 'ashes to ashes' as my mother laughed in the background. While she got a kick out of my destruction of visual reminders of fresh wounds, calling relatives to tell them what I did, one of my uncles took me aside and scolded me. He was very religious and reminded me that the man was still my father and I had to respect him. Although I stopped burning photos, that talk went in one ear and out the other. If my father didn't respect me enough to let me know what was going on why should I respect him? He gave up that privilege when he drove away that morning.

As I look back now older and wiser, though my father was dead wrong for how he conducted himself, I should have been allowed to understand exactly what was going on if I was going to be forced to choose between parents.

I had no business being a part of the conversation, however as a child you have no choice but to feel the pain and agony of the dissolution of marriage. As I said before kids are not stupid. No matter how much a parent tries to hide conflict, a child will sense something is wrong. Children stare for a reason. It is how they take in information. If a parent cries in front of their young child, that child most likely will cry as well. The same thing goes for a smile or laughter. It was this perception that allowed me to confront my father days before he left for good.

For all my deductive reasoning my parents were still my parents and all I thought about was how emotional I was that one was gone. I didn't know completely why and I didn't care. The choice was made for me without hearing my father's side of the story.

I would not speak to him again for over 15 years and because of that I had to believe my mother's side and the realization that he did not care about me. If he cared he would have come back. I held on to that belief for years, resentment building with each passing year. He was looking for me, but I would avoid him because I wasn't supposed to talk to him. As I got older it got to the point where I was fully able to assess the situation and make an informed choice of how I wanted to proceed in terms of my relationship with my father.

I chose to keep avoiding him.

What was I going to say to him? What can he say to me that would make me forgive him or keep me from ramming his head into the wall in a fit of violent, tear-soaked rage?

I didn't cry much as I got older, but I would definitely shed tears if I saw him the way I felt at the time. I had to be real with myself. I would get a nervous feeling in my stomach just hearing that he was at my aunt's house asking about me. I didn't want to give him the satisfaction of knowing that he hurt me to the point of breaking down in tears at 17 years of age. I was told that he would apologize for leaving me saying he "messed up", but that was no consolation.

For a while I thought God didn't want me to see him. There were so many instances where we barely missed crossing paths. There was the time I showed up at my aunt's house and my cousin told me my father had just left the house.

There was the other time I was walking up the street to the same house and my two cousins were outside washing the family car when they informed me my father was inside. Here was my chance to confront the man that broke up the family and failed to be a positive male role model during the critical adolescent period of my life. Here was my chance to finally hear his side of the story. Here was the opportunity I was waiting for.

What did I do?

I took a walk to the park around the corner. Before I did that, I asked my cousins to come and get me when he left.

I didn't feel bad for hiding I just didn't want to hear any excuses. The fact of the matter is there is no excuse for leaving your child. Whatever issues you have with your spouse the child is an innocent victim. Children do not ask to be here.

I had to be honest with myself. Confronting my father that day was not going to get him to drop his other woman and family and come back home with me. My mother didn't want him to know where we lived anyway. It wasn't going to be a fairytale ending and I did not know how I would feel about that. I definitely did not want to break down in front of him.

So I kept it moving.

My father's one act of walking away started a domino effect throughout my entire family that slowly split everyone apart. My extended family in Long Island had already moved to Florida by this time along with my paternal grandmother, so 32nd street was the only place left where everyone who still lived in New York came together.

With only one source of income and a rise in the monthly rent from the landlord, my mom and I moved from the two story house on East 32nd Street to an apartment on a dead-end street (the irony was not lost on me) on Chester Court between Fenimore and Rutland roads off the busy main street of Flatbush Avenue.

This was starting over. My mom ultimately took on the role of mother and father, making sure I was clothed, fed, and went to school without missing a beat. Let's be clear: my mother did a fantastic job raising me. With all the statistics showing how young Black males without a father figure turn to a life of crime, get locked up, or become addicted to drugs and alcohol, I am proud to say I never even thought about going down that path.

As I mentioned earlier my mother was a strict woman. All of five foot three inches she put the fear of God in me to the point I was terrified to do anything out of line. I also had enough respect for her to not want to disappoint her by doing something stupid.

Respect is key. A lot of kids don't respect their parents nowadays. Some parents would rather be friends with their children instead of a figure of authority. Similar to a substitute teacher in school, if a child doesn't respect you as a parent expect to be tuned out and talked over.

My mother made sure she let me know that she expected to be called whenever I reached a destination or I was coming home after the time she expected. One night I came home and found her crying in the living room. She was upset because she called all my friend's houses and she couldn't reach me. I had been with my friends, but we were walking the streets. It got a little too late in the evening for her taste and it was dark outside. I believe I was 14 at the time and the only people that had cell phones were the people portrayed by Wesley Snipes in the movie *New Jack City*.

Seeing my mother freak out like that made me understand how important it was to her that she know that I am alright at all times. I was in no danger, but she did not know that. Although I did not want to see her crying it felt good to know that she cared.

As parents I believe kids need to know that you care about their well-being. Be annoying, the point will get across. Kids subconsciously look to their parent(s)for cues on how to treat people which ultimately translates to how they approach their own children in the future.

My mom tried her best to make sure I was partaking in activities that my father should have been setting up for me. She saw to it that I was able to play little league baseball. Baseball was my favorite sport next to bowling. I grew up watching the New York Mets right along with my dad. I recall many weekends where I would see him in the living room with the Mets game on and I would sit next to him and eventually fell in love with the team and the game itself.

It also helped that the Mets were the talk of New York during the '80s. Players like Dwight "Doc" Gooden, Darryl Strawberry, Keith

Hernandez, Gary Carter, and the like stayed on the back pages of the local newspapers, not that other team. It is always amusing to me how Yankees "fans" can never recall this period of time in New York history, but I digress.

One of my fondest memories was being awakened by loud screaming coming from my parents' room. They were watching Game 6 of the 1986 National League Championship Series (NLCS) between the Mets and the Houston Astros. The game went 16 innings, I believe with the Mets winning in dramatic fashion as had been their forte.

I saw my mom and dad at the edge of their bed glued to the television with the excitement of kids opening gifts at Christmas. I could not helped but be equally enthusiastic just off their energy alone. At one point it dawned on me to look at the clock and I swore I saw 3:50 in the a.m. but I could be wrong. There was no way a baseball game could last that long could it?

Looking back I realize why my parents were so excited. Winning that game 6 clinched a berth in the World Series for New York, a title they would eventually secure in equally memorable fashion including, ironically, a similarly iconic game 6 victory over the Boston Redsox.

My goal of playing organized baseball was realized at 12 years old as a first baseman and right fielder for the North Highway Lions. It was more special because I was able to play on the same team with my boy Douglas. He was a starting pitcher on the team. I fashioned myself as a hitter after then Atlanta Braves slugger Ron Gant. I had a lot of power in my skinny frame yet I hit seventh in the lineup. That is how balanced our team was.

Being a part of the Lions was everything I thought it would be. The experience of rooting for your teammates, hitting homeruns against the opposing team's best pitcher, stealing bases, making great plays in the field, that season meant the world to me. I was doing something I loved and I was being productive. As one dream of growing with my father died, another, albeit on a much lesser scale, dream of mine came true. It wasn't the *Bonnies*, but I was playing baseball.

I will forever admire and be appreciative of my mother's strength raising a pre-teen on her own. With her guidance I was able to finish high school and graduate with a Bachelor's degree without any hardship. She helped me buy my first car brand new off the lot in 2001.

My mother was great to me, but I needed to learn how to be a man from a man. If my father had no choice and was put out because he decided to stop contributing to the marriage financially it served him right, but with that knowledge maybe our relationship would have been different. Maybe I would have walked into my aunt's house to see him instead of hiding in the park.

During my critical adolescent period, my mother could only do so much. I became overly dependent, spoiled even, a true momma's boy (even though I hated when people called me that). Being raised from one parental perspective whether you are a boy or girl is not always healthy.

CHAPTER 8

GOLDEN ERA

Those who saw the documentary released in March of 2011 on ESPN of *The Fab Five*, saw the "Five" Jalen Rose, Juwan Howard, Chris Webber, Jimmy King and Ray Jackson shout out the different music they were listening to on the road. Of the groups mentioned *EPMD, Compton's Most Wanted, N.W.A*, and *Public Enemy* were in their heavy rotation.

The era from 1986-1994, widely known as the "golden era" of Hip Hop, produced a lot of classic, fun-loving, music that defined the genre from groups like *Kid n' Play, Eric B & Rakim* and solo artists *Big Daddy Kane, M.C. Lyte, Queen Latifah* and *Slick Rick*. To a generation of youth Hip Hop was the soundtrack of their lives.

The golden era also spawned a plethora of artists with an affinity to speak on the inequities in the communities they were raised in. Groups like the aforementioned *Public Enemy* spoke out against institutionalized racism, political and social injustice, whereas *Queen Latifah* championed the plight of women with her hit singles *"Ladies First"* and *"U.N.I.T.Y."*

From the inception of the MC, the lyrics have reflected their environment. The golden era was also a period where artists were known to take chances in their music, touching on subject matter that didn't conform to what was popular.

Parenthood was a very important topic in Hip Hop music. The year 1991 spawned *Tupac Shakur's* classic *"Brenda's Got A Baby"*, a song that follows a teenage prostitute who gets pregnant and leaves her newborn baby in the dumpster, *Naughty By Nature's "Ghetto Bastard" (see Appendix i.)*, group leader *Treach*'s account of growing up without a father, and *Ed O.G. & Da Bulldogs "Be A Father to Your Child" (see Appendix i.)*, a scathing admonishment to so-called "deadbeat dads". The aforementioned songs all appeared on the debut albums of all three artists, showing the importance of speaking on real issues without regard for how their respective record sales would be affected.

Most recently, superstar hip hop artists like *Jay-Z, Nas* and *Common* have incorporated fatherhood in their music. Brooklyn-born artist *Jay-Z* regularly mentioned the pain he felt when his father left his family when he was a young boy and the effect it had on how he became a man and his relationships with women. Songs like *"Where Have You Been"* off of his 2000 album *The Dynasty* showcased a scarred and angry Shawn Carter (Jay-Z's real name) reliving the painful years growing up without the man he once thought of as his hero, questioning whether the man remembered his birthday among other things. The track is made even more poignant by the song-stealing cameo turned in by a tearful *Beanie Siegel* who claims his father "turned him out."

The late *Notorious B.I.G.* had harsh words for his father on his debut when he spit: "ready to die why I act that way/ pop duke left mom duke the faggot took the back way…" The father-son relationship in Hip Hop was not all caustic. *Nas* who was estranged from his father kept up enough of a cordial relationship to allow the jazz musician a solo on *"Life's A Bitch"* off of his debut *Illmatic* and a duet on *Streets Disciple*. *Nas* also came full circle espousing his views as a father with a song called *"Daughters"* off his *"Life Is Good"* LP. "God's Son", as he called himself, spoke directly to his own baby girl turned young lady revealing that his example wasn't the greatest yet he wanted her to make wise decisions when dealing with the opposite sex nonetheless.

Common let his dad freestyle at the end of two of his albums and *Jay-Z* finally made amends with his terminally ill father before he passed.

I have to say the golden era was my favorite time in Hip Hop music. I wish it could have lasted forever, but it would be more than naïve to think so. To use the sports analogy (because I love music and sports if you haven't noticed already), the superstars of the '80s got older and eventually had to step aside for the younger generation. Jordan had to retire (finally) at some point and move over for the LeBron James and Carmelo Anthony's of the world. Kobe is retiring at the end of the 2015-16 season making way for Stephen Curry and James Harden to lead the NBA for next decade. Well it is the same in Hip Hop. The music is ever-changing and while *A Tribe Called Quest*, *Wu-Tang Clan* and others from the era do not have the same impact with the younger audience, *Kanye West, Kendrick Lamar* and *Drake* are three artists that enjoy commercial success with golden era rhyme skill sensibilities.

When I wasn't rocking my pink shirt and leather jeans, begging my mother to buy me a pair of penny loafers, or trying to moonwalk all thanks to the influence of the incomparable, legendary *Michael Jackson*, I was playing the self-titled first album of Hip Hop group *Run-DMC* on a regular basis.

Was there violent crime and drug use going on at this time? Sure, but rappers wanted to focus on having a good time, on showing you their rhyme skills were better than yours, that their DJ was the best on the turntables, that their crew could dance circles around your crew, that their piece was an end to end burner immortalized for the boroughs to see on the side of a red number 2 train.

One of the founding fathers of Hip Hop music *Afrika Bambaataa* saw Hip Hop as a positive alternative to the gang lifestyle he was leading and influenced countless other gang members to change their way of life through the formation of the Mighty Zulu Nation.

The aforementioned *Run-DMC* and *Jam Master Jay* with their effortless back and forth rhyme style, *Big Daddy Kane*: the lyrical

95

master known for devastating punch lines and jamming consecutive rhyming words into a single line, *LL Cool J*: the architect of the first hip hop ballad *("I Need Love")* and battle rap extraordinaire, *Slick Rick*: the British-accented master of the storytelling rhyme style, *Special Ed*: the "youngest in charge" from Brooklyn, *MC Lyte*: leading the charge for the female MC with hard hitting battle raps and swagger, *Kid N' Play*: the fun-loving duo that made the kick-step dance a phenomenon and led the charge for Hip Hop expansion into the mainstream, were the Hip Hop acts I grew up on in the 1980s.

These artists and others made me fall in love with Hip Hop. They made me want to rhyme – and I did, starting out with my own fictional *Run-DMC*-inspired trio of rappers. I wrote rhymes for the two MC's and recited them over the lyrics of the real group. It was a hobby that no one in my family knew about. I was a creative kid - to that point I had been drawing my own comic books based on the *Archie* comics I loved to read and *The Real Ghostbusters* cartoon I loved to watch on Saturday mornings.

They say during your teenage years is when you try to figure out what you want to do with your life. I had that timetable beat as a pre-teen. I was caught between wanting to be an illustrator, playwright, or MC.

What does Hip Hop have to do with this conversation of fatherhood? Besides the aforementioned examples of artists who bring the importance of fatherhood and the effect of not having a father into their music, Hip Hop practically raised me. Hip Hop has raised a lot of people from single family homes or from the wrong side of the tracks. For those kids in California who were going through hard times, *N.W.A* spoke to their pain and struggle. Conversely, the videos off *The Chronic* showed there wasn't all negativity out West. The visuals of cookouts, volleyball games, and house parties was representative of people who didn't have a lot of money, but still used what they had to come together and enjoy themselves.

The *"I Got It Made"* video by *Special Ed* showed Hip Hop dancing at its finest. You knew that if you were at a party you had to be up on *The Whop*, *Cabbage Patch*, and *James Brown*.

As I mentioned in a previous chapter, many of the stories told in Hip Hop were those of people the artists knew. Hip Hop gave a voice to the voiceless. The ability to relate to a song, whether it's speaking on crime, looking for love, or not having a father, makes it an instant favorite. You either become a fan of the artist, the music as a whole, or you aspire to be a performer.

Hip Hop is not and can never replace my father. However, when my father left the home instead of rebel by hitting the streets and doing something illegal I rebelled on paper. For me personally Hip Hop music allowed me to use my time creatively.

Call me weird, but my love for writing and Hip Hop prepared me for the unexpected loss of my father. After the initial shock it was my newfound hobby that kept my mind occupied to the point I stopped thinking about him.

Thankfully by 1989 I was so enamored by Hip Hop culture all I saw was the day I would be collaborating on a track with *Kane*, *Lyte*, *LL* or *A Tribe Called Quest*. So I worked toward that goal.

I wanted to go to school in part to see my friends so we could battle rap or play roles in our favorite posse cuts like *"Scenario"* (I was always *Q-Tip*). There were times that if I wasn't writing raps in my room I would be reading a magazine like *The Source*. Writing rhymes kept me off the streets and out of trouble.

I lived through all the phases of Hip Hop post-*Sugar Hill Gang* and I am happy for it. I could not imagine being a youngster in this day and age thinking *Soulja Boy* and *Lil' Wayne* is better than *Tribe*, *Rakim*, or *Slick Rick* in his prime.

How could I not remember when I first heard Biggie's song *"Juicy"* blaring out the radio on the second floor of Dr. Jay's in the Fulton Mall Downtown Brooklyn in the summer of 1994? Then going outside and hearing *"Unbelievable"* playing out of a bootlegger's radio on Fulton Street and thinking 'that beat is ridiculous'!

I can't imagine not being around to walk 20 blocks down Flatbush Avenue to a record store in November of 1993 to buy the *"Midnight*

Marauders" **album** the day it came out and purchase another copy of "*The Low End Theory*" cassette tape I lost in Jamaica, or being too young to know about the video to "*The Symphony*".

I'm not sure if my father would have stuck around if I would have followed in his footsteps and become an electrician. In the ten years he was in my life about the last three of those were spent writing and drawing. I had a lively imagination which, combined with my passion for reading and love of cartoons, made for a lot of creative output.

While other kids learned to spell and write letters in second grade, I was forming the half-oval outline of the eyes and the small nose of *Archie* and his friends adding my own dialogue in small bubbles at the side or above their heads. "*The **Gutbusters***" were running the streets of Gotham with their own form of proton packs ridding the streets of paranormal activity.

For some reason at such a young age I loved shows that were before my time. My weeknights and days during summer vacation were spent watching shows like *I Love Lucy*, *The Monkees*, *I Dream of Jeannie*, *Happy Days, Three's Company* and more. This was before the daytime airwaves were dominated by talk shows and the evenings by reality programming.

My all-time favorite show from a bygone era was *The Honeymooners*. Although the shenanigans of bus driver Ralph Kramden his wife Alice, his best friend Ed Norton and Ed's wife

99

Trixie debuted in 1952 and was the influence for a little cartoon named *The Flintstones*, I stayed up way past my bedtime to catch the nightly hilarity. The show inspired me so much that as a nine year-old I began writing the aforementioned original plays based on the show.

Don't get me wrong I loved playing outside with my friends as much as anybody, but my fun came with restrictions: I couldn't play in the street or leave the block (until I was nine). I was also one of millions of kids whose mother stuck her head out (in my case over the patio railing) and yelled for me to come inside when it got dark. My late evenings and nights were occupied perfecting my craft.

My aspirations of being a rap star were years away at that point only becoming serious after a missed opportunity to kick lyrics for a certain legendary female MC who knew my sister from junior high school. She had come by the apartment my mother and I were staying in at the time in 1991 to pick up my sister and bring her to Penn Station. My sister was on her way back to Delaware State University and this famous MC took the time to stop by our little apartment to see an old friend.

That's keeping it real. She knew me and my mom from those days with my sister in junior high school. That familiarity ironically made me hesitant to share my talent.

'I'm sure she has a bunch of people running up to her trying to kick raps,' I thought.

'She is on her leisure time right now, I don't want to bother her with music stuff,' I reasoned to myself.

And finally 'am I good enough to impress her?' was the million dollar question I posed to myself.

Even back then I was too hard on myself, my worst critic as the saying goes. My impromptu critique of my own skills kept me quiet that evening, even as I sat in the superstar's jeep as we waited for my sister to come outside. She was listening to music. It was someone's demo tape.

"What do you think?" she asked.

"Sounds good," I opined.

No it wasn't. Truth was I didn't hear anything but noise. I was still wondering why I was stopping myself from spitting my lyrics. The worst she could say was "no". And that is exactly what I didn't want to hear. It probably would have crushed me, sent me in the opposite direction completely.

As it were I let the female MC drive off with my sister that evening. As her jeep rumbled away into the noise that was Flatbush Avenue I immediately regretted my decision. I think I went in my room and wrote like three rhymes that night. That desire turned into a passion to get better, fueling my hunger as I went into battle with schoolmates on the B60 bus riding to and from Philippa Schuyler Intermediate School, into a circle of kids all familiar with each other from Bildersee Junior High in a cafeteria in Canarsie High School, and in a Morgan State dorm room never afraid to spit when I had to.

The golden era of Hip Hop made me want to be a Hip Hop artist. 1993 and 1994 were the best years post-West Coast dominance for me. Late in '93 the *Wu-Tang Clan* dropped *Enter the Wu-Tang*, *A Tribe Called Quest* released *Midnight Marauders*, *Black Moon* came out hard with *Enta Da Stage* and '94 saw the likes of *Nas*, *The Notorious B.I.G.*, *O.C.* and *Jeru the Damaja* drop classic debuts. *Redman* spazzed out on *Dare Iz A Darkside* and *Method Man* led an onslaught of solo albums from the Wu with *Tical*.

My rhyme skills landed me on the *Freestyle Friday* segment of *BET's 106 and Park* for three weeks in March of 2001. A lot of my friends saw me, as well as a lot of my family all the way in Jamaica. But did my father see me? Did anyone bother to tell him that I was on TV?

I didn't think about it then, but once again I achieved personal success and my father wasn't around to see it. This time I would not be coming home to tell him the story.

CHAPTER 9

THE NBA CARES

"the streets is a short stop/ either you slinging crack rock or you got a wicked jump shot"[7]

Similar to actors and rappers, most urban youth in the 1990s aspired to be NBA athletes. During this time Michael Jordan dazzled basketball courts throughout the league having many people wanting to *"Be Like Mike"* as his popular advertising campaign for Gatorade sports drinks suggested.

As professional basketball icons Larry Bird and Magic Johnson (widely credited with bringing the NBA back to the forefront of sports entertainment in the 1980s) retired, the rekindled popularity of the NBA had a lot of urban youth in the gym or on the street courts trying to emulate Magic's otherworldly passes, Bird's effortless jump shot, or Jordan's dazzling array of moves such as the "Air" reverse layup.

---

[7] Notorious B.I.G., "Things Done Changed", 1994

For kids without a father in the home, playing a sport and, by extension, being part of a team made all the difference in the world. For most urban youth the game of choice was basketball. The coach of the team provided discipline and direction that not only involved the game. If he really went above and beyond, the coach would be someone the youngster could talk to about anything.

With God-given physical gifts of height and hand-eye coordination, these kids would get an opportunity to go to college that would probably be unavailable otherwise. Beginning in 1996 highly talented kids began to pass up college and enter the NBA draft straight out of high school. The move had been made less than a handful of times in league history – Moses Malone, Shawn Kemp and Kevin Garnett being the last to successfully make the jump in the 20 years prior – yet being so close to fulfilling a lifelong dream is difficult to resist.

Let's face it these youth come from nothing, living in the projects, mother struggling with two or three jobs to support multiple children, father sweating in the backyard teaching the fundamentals of the game, knocking them down and preparing them for the rigors of competition. Being a high draft pick in the NBA promised an immediate end to any financial hardship. What child wouldn't want to repay their parents for all the love they showed?

I wish I would have kept playing baseball, but I stopped once I got to high school. Why? I didn't want to stay after school for practice.

The same with football. I was a great player in junior high, albeit without pads I still had a great set of hands, speed and the ability to avoid rival defenders. Maybe if I would have ended up at the same high school as my friends I would have joined the team along with them, the whole being part of a team family concept.

I did try out for the varsity basketball team in high school along with 60 other people. There were only 15 spots available and I had seen more than 30 of the guys trying out play on the street courts and knew they were better than I was. When it was my time to try out, I missed a point blank layup at the rim the only time I touched the ball. I was deflated. I just knew I was definitely not making the team so I did not show up the following week for final cut.

I am not going to beat the lesson here over your head, but just know that ultimately 45 guys that tried out that day got cut because they had bad grades. Out of the guys that made the school team I was better than five of them hands down. Who knows if I had not eliminated myself I would have made that team and possibly gone further. I had a great jump shot and drive to the basket. Playing with that team would have demanded that I shore up my dribbling and left hand. Maybe I could have gone further and helped change my mother's living situation.

If you look at the NBA drafts of the mid to late '90s, the majority of the top prospects were at Madison Square Garden with their mother. Their mother was the first person they kissed as their name was called. Look at the 1996 draft for a moment (arguably the greatest draft ever). The first overall pick was Allen Iverson; no father in the camera shot, only his biggest supporter: his mother Ann.

Stephon Marbury, the fourth pick in the 1996 draft, was an example of a kid from a tough neighborhood (Coney Island area of Brooklyn, New York) who came from a large family of siblings who played basketball. In fact Marbury and his older brothers were all high school legends on the hardwood, but never made it to the league until Stephon's name was called by David Stern.

The emotional family hug that followed said it all. Marbury instantly became the savior of the family. Making the NBA immediately made their situation improve and the tears of joy showed how relieved they all were. This was the story for many urban youth who played team sports to take their mind off of their living condition or to be a part of a team of guys that became a support system, if not family.

In 2003 LeBron James was the first overall pick in the NBA draft. When his name was called he kissed his mother Gloria. Again, there was no father around. LeBron's pick at the draft was a culmination of years of media hype including some calling him "The Chosen One", being given the nickname "King James", and signing a $90 million contract with shoe giant Nike before playing an NBA game.

It may seem like LeBron was spoon fed, but he earned all of his accolades based on his remarkable basketball skills. His mother gave birth to him at sixteen, they were on their own three years later living off of food stamps. The camaraderie LeBron had with his St. Vincent St. Mary's high school teammates is documented on film. That was his family.

The NBA saw an influx of predominantly Black players coming into the NBA in the '90s and early 2000s because these kids were the best players available. Still many criticized the changing of the culture of the league. There were a ton of news stories circulating in the media about Black NBA athletes getting arrested for drug or weapons possession, driving while intoxicated, having altercations in public places and fathering multiple children with different women.

These indiscretions, along with the infamous 2004 "Malice at the Palace" melee where then-Indiana Pacers forward Ron Artest went into the crowd in Detroit after being hit with a cup of beer while lying on the scorer's table, led journalists like SportsIllustrated.com writer Pete McEntegart to write in his February 23rd 2005 installment of *"10 Spot"* that "a number of NBA observers" called the NBA a "Hip Hop league".

These "observers" were criticizing the halftime show of the NBA All-Star Game that year that featured country music stars. Whether it was meant in a negative way or not the term stuck, used condescendingly as more teenagers made the leap from high school into the NBA bringing the urban fashion, accessories, and brash personality into the league with them.

Obviously not every player in the league carried themselves like Iverson (who had a brief attempt at a rap career). It just so happens most of the players love Hip Hop music. They grew up on Hip Hop music and it is the soundtrack of their lives. Music as a whole has the power to get the biggest celebrities and the ordinary citizen through the toughest times. Everyone has a go-to song so to speak when you're happy, heartbroken, or just feel the need to relax.

While African-American athletes were more inclined to play basketball or football, Caucasian and Latin-American athletes were more inclined to play baseball. Evidence of the decline in Black baseball players in the Major Leagues led to an initiative started by Philadelphia Phillies slugger Ryan Howard called "R.B.I." (a baseball term for Runs Batted In) Revitalizing Baseball in Inner cities, to foster the interest of baseball in more African-Americans.

The influx of Asian athletes into the Major Leagues in the late '90s has been well documented; however the MLB has never been referred to as a "kung-fu league". This would be seen as irresponsible, not to mention racist and insensitive.

So why can the NBA get called a "Hip Hop league", a glaring stereotype accepted so much so that superstar athletes such as Allen Iverson, Latrell Sprewell, Ron Artest, and Jermaine O'Neal can be given as examples of this "change for the worse"?

It is my belief that it didn't do so much with the style of dress as with the fact that there were little to no Caucasian superstars in the vein of a Larry Bird that middle-aged fans could call their own. Talent is talent no matter the color, or style of dress. Iverson's gaudy chains, tattoos and baseball cap weren't standard uniform off the court, but on the court Iverson played as hard as Bird ever did driving the lane with reckless abandon getting knocked down seemingly each time. Iverson's heart could never be questioned and should not have been downplayed because he wore his newfound wealth all over his body.

It was Allen Iverson's personal style and he had a right to express his individuality. The 21st century NBA is obviously not the same as the 1980s. The same way the 24-hour information age of the 21st century is totally different than 30 years ago these players were not going to wear short shorts or let their hair fall out and not cut it completely off.

Like anything in life, change is inevitable and even if the "NBA observers" McEntegart wrote about did not mean any harm in their generalization, there were people who felt "their" league was being taken over.

One of the ubiquitous criticisms journalists levied on the NBA during the '90s was the influence the behavior of its athletes was having on children. In response, Charles Barkley, currently an NBA analyst on the TNT cable network program *Inside the NBA*, then a member of the Phoenix Suns appeared in an ad for major apparel giant Nike. In the ad Barkley claimed:

"I am not a role model…parents should be role models…just because I can dunk a basketball, doesn't mean I should raise your kids."

At the time this commercial aired I watched it and thought nothing of it, mainly because I thought it was silly. I never looked at an athlete as someone I expected to teach me right from wrong. I had a mother who would beat me with a leather belt while I was soaking wet as a reminder I need not do anything stupid (that may be considered child abuse today, but back then it was called discipline). That athlete went through his/her own trials and tribulations to get where they are. His/her job is to play the respective sport at a high level and earn the money he/she is being paid. No different than the average working citizen, save for the notoriety being on television brings.

Barkley took the stance that athletes are not responsible for teaching children right from wrong, that it was the job of the parent to effectively instill moral fiber in the child. The media backlash was instant, attacking Barkley's remarks as irresponsible.

According to the critics, kids look up to NBA athletes and in turn the athletes are expected to conduct themselves in a professional manner. A true statement, but Barkley's point, as I saw it, is that parents should be who children look up to. Once their favorite NBA athlete retires, who will be their hero then? A parent can be a child's hero for a lifetime.

In the very same commercial Barkley had on sneakers that became very popular with young people. Why? Because Barkley was having the season of his career in Phoenix. Regardless of your familial situation kids still have favorite sports athletes who they emulate or aspire to be. I'm sure Barkley did not mind that his signature shoe sold well then and has since comeback in style as part of the retro sneaker movement.

Conversely, the suit and tie sensibility of Michael Jordan (who's heart on a basketball court can never be questioned), a look he said was important to project to the people waiting to see him before and after games, showed how seriously he took his superstar status and the importance of being responsible in how you carry yourself.

Arguably the greatest professional basketball player ever, Jordan was heavily influenced by his father. Who was by Jordan's side every time he won a championship during his first three-peat with the Chicago Bulls? It wasn't his wife. It wasn't his mother. Look back at the locker room celebration of Jordan's first championship in 1991 and there is Jordan's father James holding his son's shoulders as he leaned his head into the Larry O'Brien trophy and cried his heart out.

At his most vulnerable moment, shedding tears of relief at finally reaching his goal after years of being told he could never win as a scorer, after years of being vanquished by the Boston Celtics and then the Detroit Pistons in brutal fashion, Jordan wanted his father.

When James Jordan was tragically slain in 1993, Jordan retired from the game he dominated to play baseball. Jordan faced enormous and harsh criticism for taking up minor league baseball, a sport he had not played since he was in high school, but worked just as hard to try to make it to the Major Leagues in honor of his father who Jordan said always wanted him to play professionally.

When he returned to basketball, leading the Bulls to the most wins in NBA history (72) and winning his fourth championship on Father's Day in 1996, Jordan was again overcome with emotion.

In one of the most memorable locker room scenes in history, Jordan can be seen face down on the floor alone with only the game ball at his head violently sobbing such that his body shook. Why? His father wasn't there to celebrate the NBA championship with him for the first time ever. The reality of the senselessness of the murder of a child's hero, the violent separation of a close-knit family had set in.

The NBA has recently taken great strides to clean up their image in the public by reinforcing a dress code for players, the *"where amazing happens"* campaign highlighting great moments on the court, and the *NBA Cares* initiative showing NBA players doing charitable work such as building houses, reading to children, and serving food at homeless shelters.

NBA players have exposed their family life to the public showing they are responsible family men as well. Stars like Shaquille O'Neal opened his home to MTV Cribs, in 2008 the WNBA - the female version of the NBA - utilized then-Detroit Pistons starting point guard Chauncey Billups flanked by his two young daughters in their commercials promoting the upstart league, and Phoenix Suns superstar Grant Hill did a special for MTV called "24 Hours With..." that showed what a whirlwind a day in his life is juggling spending quality time with his two daughters, supporting his wife, recording artist Tamia, and practicing with his team.

Speaking of Grant Hill, one of the most controversial moments of the ESPN documentary *The Fab Five*, the film based on the five Black freshman that went to the University of Michigan in the fall of 1991 and started for the varsity basketball team that year leading the school to two straight NCAA title games, was when Jalen Rose called Hill who played for rival Duke University an "Uncle Tom".

The comment, which pretty much has the same effect on a Black man as the "n" word, sparked a heated debate on whether Black men who attend Duke should apologize for going to the school. Duke is a perennial college basketball power due to the quality of players recruited by coach Mike Krzyzewski. Black players who have attended Duke and gone on to the NBA such as Elton Brand, and Shane Battier among others can never be mistaken for "dumb jocks". Although they were brought to Duke for their amazing basketball ability these were well-spoken young men who steered clear of controversy.

With all the pain I felt going through my issues with my father, my suffering has occurred to this point in relative obscurity. There is nothing worse than having a father who is a public figure abandon you. This is what Jalen Rose had to endure growing up in the projects of Detroit. His father played in the NBA, yet Rose grew up poor.

On the other hand Grant Hill's father Calvin was a star player in the National Football League. His mother Janet went to school with former First Lady and Secretary of State and current Presidential candidate Hillary Clinton. Rose could not understand why his father could not be like Calvin Hill, able to be a husband and father while juggling the demands of a pro sport. Rose took out his anger on a team he felt was full of spoiled players. He clearly stated his resentment was for Grant Hill's privileged two-parent upbringing, a sentiment he no longer holds true as a mature adult, yet the damage was seemingly done.

Grant Hill took out a public column in the New York Times to voice his displeasure over being called a "sellout". Hill should not have to apologize because his father decided to stick around and he had the opportunity to go to one of the best schools. He is a better man for his upbringing and one of the classiest gentlemen the NBA has seen. As I mentioned in the preface the best revenge is to make something out of yourself. Rose went on to forge his own respectable NBA career and is currently one of the more entertaining NBA analysts on ESPN. He is also giving back to his Detroit community with his eponymous Jalen Rose Leadership Academy which opened in the fall of 2011.

Working at a hotel where the NBA Draft prospects have stayed I had the honor of meeting players like New Orleans Hornets point guard Chris Paul, Chicago Bulls superstar and 2011 NBA MVP Derrick Rose, and others before they were drafted. I checked in Al Horford and met his mother and father, I witnessed Rudy Gay's family celebrate in the lobby after returning from the draft where he was picked by the Memphis Grizzlies.

One moment I remember vividly, however, was former Portland Trailblazers superstar Brandon Roy's father the morning after his son was drafted. He came to the desk wearing the Trailblazers hat a little before 6 a.m. As is customary I asked if everything was okay with his stay and seeing his hat inquired if he had a good time at the draft. I will never forget how wide his smile was as he said "we're going to Portland."

I witnessed a proud father beaming with pride over a boy that he raised finally achieving his dream. It is a beautiful thing to see. In the 2011 NBA draft a father's diligence paid off in the number one pick Kyrie Irving (another Duke product). I mentioned previous number one draft picks with no male presence to turn to when their name was called, but Irving turned to only one man when his name was called by Commissioner David Stern: his father Drederick.

At the time of the draft Drederick had been raising the 19 year-old Kyrie as a single dad for 15 years after the tragic death of his wife and Kyrie's mom Elizabeth. Drederick, a former star at Boston University, was instrumental in teaching his son the fundamentals of basketball and inspiring Kyrie's drive and dedication to the sport that allowed him to impress the Cleveland Cavaliers enough to use the number one pick on the 6'4" point guard after only 11 games of college ball at Duke.

It was two years prior that dad played with his son in an AAU pick-up game against other high school kids and showed flashes of his "old school" college brilliance throwing down two-handed slams and chest bumping his son. The younger Irving also earned his stripes playing and losing to his dad in one-on-one games until finally breaking through once he grew to his current height and his arms got too long for dad to box with.

A story like this is awe-inspiring and shows the impact of the Black father on his progeny. The fact that he endured the death of the love of his life as a 30 year-old and still found the courage to remain a strong example for his child for the past decade and a half illustrates the selflessness and inner strength that has been passed on to Kyrie not only as a point guard, but as a person. Drederick made sure his son felt the love of his mother while teaching him life lessons of perseverance.

The NBA has done well in cleaning up its image from the early 2000s, but there is no substitute for the impact a devoted mother or father has on a young kid trying to become the next great sports superstar.

CHAPTER 10

STEP, POPS!

One thing that would make a child resent an absentee father more is a stepfather, a stepfather from hell that is. To any child that loses his biological father, any man that steps into that role would be the father from hell. He could be the nicest person in the world, even nicer than your real father and part of you will still yearn for the original simply because he was there first, unless of course the original was a monster. The way I felt, if my stepfather was the alternative, I would learn to forgive my father real quick.

The child isn't the only person that suffers when a father is not present. The mother and, in most cases, wife or girlfriend goes through agonizing pain and, depending on how the split happened and who the father ended up with, a sense of betrayal, emotional distress and devastating insecurity.

I witnessed all of the above when my father decided to leave. My mother cried - a lot. The waterworks came at unexpected times, but frequently. One such breakdown came after she came home from work. I was already home from school with my older sister. My mother walked into the living room area to greet us and sat down on the sofa. Without warning she broke into a chorus of uncontrollable sobs. My sister and I looked at each other stunned at the randomness of the outburst. My sister extended a sympathetic shoulder to cry on as I looked on stoically. There was nothing I could do to take away my mother's pain right then or over the next year for that matter.

****

The most difficult thing for a child to bear next to the departure of a parent is when the remaining parent moves on to a new relationship. If it were up to me my mother would stay single forever, but that was not realistic. Once I came to accepting the thought of another man shacking up with my mother, then I had to deal with her choices.

I approached the situation with an open mind, as long as my mother was happy and could take her mind off of my father - who I was calling "him" by this time - I was okay. But was I really? Why did it even have to come to this? I was on a first name basis with my father and now I was using a pronoun to identify him.

There was the guy who my mother met at one of my second cousin's infamous New Year's Eve parties. I wasn't as hard on him as I thought I would be, my only issue being that he smoked like a chimney, or so I thought.

He tried too hard to ingratiate himself to me by driving me to my Little League games. I can't recall if it was a Chevy, but I remember the car was blue, it was long and it made a loud noise when it drove off from a stop position.

After all the years we watched New York Mets games on the living room floor, my parents' excitement during the classic 1986 marathon playoff game between the Mets and the Houston Astros, and my desire to play with the Bonnies, I was playing real baseball and my father wasn't there.

I looked at the parking area a few yards away from the diamond I was playing on in the Marine Park section of Brooklyn and my mother's boyfriend was leaning on his car smoking a cigarette and smiling. He didn't care about what I was doing. Sure he tried to look like he gave a damn, but how else could he make sure I didn't meddle in his personal affairs with my mother?

The only person that smoked around me was our landlord at East 32nd street, but that was when I was around the man, which was usually not a lot. At least he smoked outside the house. This guy would light up in the apartment. I don't know, I didn't really dig coming out of my room and seeing haze from floating cigarette smoke. The fact that this was acceptable in the house around me, a young child of 12 at the time, was troubling.

I remember bringing up this point in a conversation with my mother that got heated. I believe I mentioned the possibility that the guy was using her. I was never a sour grapes sort of child, but I wasn't stupid. The guy was blatantly trying to buy my affection and I never brought that part up. If he didn't smoke I would have probably kept my mouth shut, but I was dying a slow death. I couldn't take it.

She was in denial, an unfortunately normal reaction. The raw emotion of losing the love of your life sometimes leads to bad judgment when a woman enters a new relationship. Far too often women bring new men into their family totally disregarding how it affects the child. Only three of my uncles on both sides of my entire family smoke, so for my mother to get into a relationship with a man that did that was way out of character for her.

My mother's reaction angered me and predictably "smoke guy" turned out to be a bum. I never said I told her so, I was glad he was gone and I hoped she would be more careful when entering a new relationship and not sell herself short.

****

The first time I met the man who would become my mother's second husband, I had a bad feeling. First off I didn't trust any strange man after the crap the last guy put my mother through. To me the only good thing about this guy was that he did not pull out a cigarette. Who knows what he said to warrant the next step, meeting the family. Hell, I didn't even know my mother was seeing anybody new and that gave me a feeling of déjà vu.

In some strange way I felt betrayed. I felt like I was being force fed. The man already made it to the apartment so I had no say in the matter. He was already "in there" - the smirk on his face confirmed that. I was supposed to be the man of the house. That's how it was for six years to that point. Was I going to have to call this strange man "dad"? He never took me to McDonalds, he wasn't the man that taught me how to ride a bike, picking me up every time I lost my balance and fell into the bushes.

'How dare my mother just bring this guy into the house and expect me to accept it,' I thought.

Needless to say my anger got the best of me that evening and I ended up ripping my shirt open in a fit of rage in front of our guest and storming out of the living room area.

My mother politely excused herself and made a beeline to her bedroom where I had gone. She came around that corner and hit me with the knuckle to the forehead, the same knuckles that hit me in second grade when I was stupid enough to follow a classmate off of school grounds at P.S. 235 and onto Albany Avenue only to have the Vice Principal waiting for us when we came back. I didn't know where I was going that day or what I was thinking. I was too young to think about playing hooky. I actually liked going to school at that time.

That day those knuckles felt like ten beatings. I was called out of class and into the principal's office where my mother was waiting.

She started towards me immediately, angry more because I put my safety at risk by leaving school grounds. I don't remember what she was saying to me at the time.

Have you ever had your parent whisper while they were scolding you? My mother, bless her heart, was trying not to embarrass me in the school office, but definitely wanted to get her point across that she would not tolerate me doing what I did again. She didn't pull off her belt; no I got a fate far worse: the five knuckles of death. The right hand came fast and furious at my forehead. Two knocks to the noggin and I was sent on my way back to class.

Sounds like nothing, right?

For some reason I could not stop crying for the life of me. I had my head down at my desk successfully hiding my face, but the whole class heard my unsuccessful attempts at stifling my sobs.

I didn't cry that evening. I was sixteen, but there I was tearing open my clothes like a little kid because my mother had the audacity to attempt to move on with her life. Subconsciously I was still the little ten year-old having a tantrum. I had to realize that my mother was not going to be single forever, she was too beautiful (where else do you think I got it from?).

My mother had long stopped beating me, but felt I deserved a flashback of the knuckle sandwich at that moment. It was rude of me. I had better manners than that. Truthfully I had no right to react that way. For the better part of the last three years beginning with the summer after I graduated from Philippa Schuyler middle school, I spent little time at home.

My sister was living full-time in Virginia at this point after graduating from college. Who was my mother going to talk to while I was selfishly hanging with my friends. There was nothing wrong with hanging out, but I could have come home at night. The friends I was staying with didn't have their fathers present in the home, but they weren't leaving their mothers to stay with me on a regular basis. Certainly my mother was going to get lonely. There was no Valentine's Day to celebrate or anyone to enjoy birthdays with.

I should have been upset at myself for not being more available to have the conversation about her love life and how my staying out affected her. Maybe she didn't want to discuss it with me. It is an awkward conversation to have.

I was also going through the inevitable physical changes every teenager experiences and I now realize how my mother being in transition in her love life affected me in a subtle way. When I was younger people would always say I looked like her, but as my hormones began to rage and I started to grow facial hair, family members began to say I looked like my father.

I had a thin moustache on my face as young as 12 years old. The issue was the beard that was growing in. I didn't own a razor or clippers at the time so I had no choice but to let it grow. Part of me always wanted to be older than my actual age and the new facial hair finally made me look the part.

I tried the new look in public at my cousin's wedding in 1993. I look at pictures of myself now from that day and I cringe. My moustache did not connect to my beard. All the hair grew at the sides of my face and under my chin. It did not look right to me.

My mother bought me a razor so I could shave and I cut the whole beard off. When I went to the barbershop I asked them to cut off any facial hair that grew in. I thought it was in my best interest vanity-wise, but subconsciously I did not want to look like my father.

I was aggravated when family members - especially on his side of the family - told me that I was looking more and more like him. I was finally using a razor, but I wasn't trying to be like my father, I wanted to get rid of any reminders of him.

I spent days staring at myself in the mirror trying to see what my relatives were talking about. I couldn't see a resemblance and I thought if I got rid of the facial hair they would not either.

Going through these emotional changes and having to deal with a visual reminder that we were not going to be a family again when I thought I got past those feelings was like being brought back to the summer of 1989.

I eventually walked up to this guy and extended my hand in apology. The year was 1995. The next year I went away to college and left my mother alone at home… again.

Apparently this was the opening her new man needed. When my mother bought her own home in 1997, the lines came fast and furious. To paraphrase: "You should let me move in, you shouldn't be alone in the house". I couldn't do anything to stop the inevitable. I was enjoying the independence going to college away from home brought. I mean, my mother was courteous enough to ask my sister and me for our permission to let her man move in, but come on. What were we going to say? No? She's a grown ass woman who brought us into the world.

I thought nothing of it. He was harmless, I thought. And part of me felt bad leaving my mom alone so as long as she had someone there on a regular basis I was cool. Plus I didn't plan on coming back home any time soon so I would not be subject to the guy on a daily basis. Less than two years later I was back at my mother's house.

I was really enjoying college life at Morgan State so much in terms of partying that I wasn't focusing on my school work, wasting tuition money in the process. I decided a move back to New York would be good to get my grades back on track, plus Tracy-Ann (my girlfriend at the time) was there. I'd had enough of the long distance that separated us.

****

My sister and I had surprised our mother for her 50th birthday in May of 1998. To my surprise, my mom was married.

'When did this happen?' I thought.

I was stunned and appalled among other adjectives, but the above thought came out of my mouth in a relatively calm manner. My mom informed me that the ceremony was done at a justice of the peace because she had already had her "big" wedding with my father and did not want to do that again.

'Who told you to get married again in the first place?' is what I really wanted to say.

We only gave permission for this guy to move in the house, not put a ring on my mother's finger. I wanted to grab her by the triceps and shake some sense into her.

'What were you thinking, woman?'

That visual would only remain in my daydreams. I could only put on a brave face and hope for the best.

I knew I really did not trust this guy now. Why the rush to get married? I guess subconsciously the realization hit me that my mother had officially moved on. My father blew it a long time ago, but there was no coming back now. Hell, I didn't even know if he ever wanted to come back. From what I knew he never asked for or about my mother when inquiring about me.

That was neither here nor there. There was a new man that had the title, like it or not. He was loud. He said things at times that made me cringe. I hated my father more. I felt if he would have stuck around, this guy would not be here.

For seven years my stepfather did everything my mother asked of him. She was content as she was remarried and finally had some normalcy in her life. I was there for every moment and while I was cordial – sharing views on the state of the New York Knicks without Patrick Ewing, the Nets with Jason Kidd, and other sports – I still didn't completely trust him.

I guess I was making continuous comparisons to what I had as a father and who was in the role at the present time. I was like one of those watchdog groups: PETA watching Naomi Campbell or GLAAD with an eye on Tracy Morgan. I picked apart everything, not realizing I was making mental notes. He was not as good looking as my father, he was not as athletic, so he was not good enough to take on the role of father. As I said, Denzel Washington could have been my stepfather and I still would have found something wrong with him. He simply was not the man who I grew up with and that had a surprising hold on my way of thinking.

Whenever neighbors or strangers asked if he was my father I quickly corrected them. The quick marriage and the rush to move in had rubbed me the wrong way and that impression stayed with me over the years. I did not want my mother to be taken advantage of.

I made the mistake of underestimating the strength of my mother and my tendency to play Superman and expose the villain (my stepfather) preying on her vulnerability led to a childish feud that lasted for the better part of three years.

It is a shame my mother had to be in the crossfire of this war of words, but I was beyond any kind of rational thought. I knew that I did not trust her husband and I was finally going to tell her why she should leave him.

Oh, if it were that easy.

The sewage that was directed towards me ranged from "f" bombs to being a piece of you-know-what. I had never been subject to verbal abuse before. It led me to believe my stepfather harbored a deep resentment towards me. In turn I attacked everything from his physical appearance to his driving skills, or lack thereof. Any personal faults - and there were many inside and out – I touched on them.

None of my insults affected my stepfather as much as when I told him my father was a better man than he was. He could not understand how I could say that when my father walked out on me. As I stated before my father never hit me and, most importantly, never uttered a cuss word in my direction.

Surely if I would have endured 25 years of my stepfather I would have been scarred for life. In fact I am sure of it. In actuality this incident did traumatize me. I was angry all the time, I had a hair trigger temper, and at times I was taking it out on my soon-to-be wife.

I was a spoiled child. I refused to admit this all of my life, but because of this I was expecting my mother to choose me over her husband. What I did not consider was how agonizing this situation had to be for her. She was definitely caught in the middle. She felt extreme pressure and the conflict was stressing her out. I believed getting rid of my stepfather would alleviate the stress. One thing my wife always told me is that once you get married your spouse comes first and kids second.

I certainly didn't understand that logic at the time. I was there first. My mother confirmed my sentiments by telling me my stepfather knew what he was getting into when he met her. I was part of the package. I was glad to hear that then, but in reality that was fine when I was seventeen. When I moved away to Baltimore at eighteen all bets should have been off.

As I said before I never planned on coming back to my mother's house, but I did because it did not make sense to live in a dorm at Long Island University when I could commute the half an hour distance to downtown Brooklyn and save dormitory fees.

I was too old to be anybody's package. I shouldn't have been living there, especially having a girlfriend that had her own place.

Truth-be-told, I was getting married. I was going to be leaving my mother's house just like I did when I started college eight years earlier. My mother was looking out for herself and she deserved to do that.

After everything that transpired my stepfather had the audacity to want an invite to my destination wedding a year later. Was he out of his mind? The nerve and straight gall to even think I would allow him to be there made me laugh. I had been giving him the silent treatment whenever I wasn't tossing profanities his way. The silence drove him crazy. He actually expected me to speak to him like nothing happened.

To be honest I never swore that much in my life, not even in my rap songs. Not even as a pre-teen when you just curse to hear yourself say it around your friends thinking you're cool because your parents aren't around. I definitely did not swear around women. So this guy had me way out of my element.

He wasn't invited to my wedding or the baby shower. I don't know if he was hurt by this or just upset that he couldn't be around the family. I just felt he did not deserve to be at the two biggest events in my life. It was only family and friends in attendance and I did not consider my stepfather to be either to me at that time.

My mother constantly brought him up in conversation trying to ease tensions, but I didn't want to hear anything about him and I told her as much sitting in my car one evening.

Sometimes I thought my mother was crazy. Was she on Mars the entire time? Was I really supposed to act like I cared for a man that called me out of my name with such ease? As far as I was concerned he hated my guts. He always hated me so why should I pretend like I gave a damn about his well being?

****

The day of my son's Christening I had an epiphany. I would be cordial to my stepfather upon seeing him. There was no thought process or lead up to my decision to choose that day to bury the hatchet except for the fact that my son would be visiting my mother's house - in the presence of my stepfather – and would sometimes be, if I knew my mother, alone with my stepfather.

I did not want to run the risk of my son being the target of any residual vitriol aimed at me. Besides, God talks about forgiveness. My wife was very influential in changing my outlook for the sake of the baby. The truth of the matter is there were many reasons I should have come to the conclusion I did to speak to my stepfather way before my son's Christening.

During the early morning hours of that special day, I stopped by my mother's house. The nervous feeling in my stomach was working overtime as I pulled the car to a stop. I told no one of what I was about to do, not my wife, not my mother. It had been roughly three years since the first blowup and almost two years since I stopped speaking to him completely. For all the anxiety I felt leading up to the exchange, the moment came and went quickly. A simple "good morning" as I crossed paths with him opened the floodgates.

"Good morning" escaped my stepfather's lips, the shock evident in his voice. As I headed towards the kitchen I swore I heard a sigh of relief. However literal or figurative the relief was, and I felt it too, I sensed my stepfather waited a long time for that salutation. I was all smiles that morning. My son was getting christened in the house of the Lord and I had just been the bigger person reconciling with a man twice my age.

"Jay!" my stepfather bellowed.

I swear he called me at least five different times for reasons I am sure he didn't even know now, just to see if I was really talking to him again. I believe he wanted to make sure my mother saw that I was being cordial. My speaking to him was a tremendous victory.

No matter how stubborn I was in my resolve, I had to admit that in his own unique way my stepfather had a point. A few years removed from the situation I understand that he was trying to tell me, in his own colorful language, that I needed to be a man; being 25 years old and still living with my mother was not cool. He wanted to live with his wife in their home without her grown son coming in and out, sharing auto insurance, and the like.

Although my mother would say she was always okay with me being there because I was working, and I was not drinking or doing drugs, I felt I was living off of her for way too long. Some people are fine with living with their mother deep into their 30s and 40s, but I knew to take that next step into full manhood I should have moved in with Tracy-Ann and set up a proper foundation for our life together.

This is the danger of not having a father in the household. I repeat: you have to learn to be a man from a man. My father married my mother when he was two months shy of his 21st birthday. I am positive he would have had some things to say about my relationship with Tracy-Ann.

My mother's natural instinct is to nurture me, as it should be, and many mothers fall victim to being comfortable having their children under their roof where they know they are safe.

Let the kids go, mothers! Let your sons be their own men. Listen to them and believe that they can make their own decisions. Fathers don't have that issue. For the most part they are trying to get you the hell out of the house as soon as you hit 18. Maybe I could have used that.

With daughters it's a little tricky no matter which parent is in the home. Mothers and fathers are equally protective of their daughters because of their own experiences with and around other men. Young women need just as much guidance from their fathers, not only for the birds and the bees talk, but seeing an example of a strong father will allow them to set the bar equally as high when seeking a man.

My mother never approached me to find out why I decided to let bygones be bygones with my stepfather. I think she was so relieved that she didn't want to even address the issue lest I change my mind.

I could have said "oh now you don't wanna talk about him," but I digress.

My relationship with my stepfather now is much better. I speak to him whenever I see him (he greets me with a handshake and a hug) and he has been the only grandpa that my son has known his entire life. Years later my mother is still married and my conspiracy theories about my stepfather have been thankfully unfounded. It helps that I am not living at the house anymore as well. I am glad we could both be mature and come to a common ground.

Lessons can be learned from abusive parents, but it doesn't mean a child should sit idly by and endure any kind of suffering. I was able to find the lesson behind the histrionics, but situations are very different when matters get physically, emotionally, and sexually out of control. In cases like this I would say get help first and be pensive later. Do not be afraid to tell someone you trust. It is NEVER your fault.

That went way left, but I did say I would look at all situations, and abuse is very real for a lot of kids living with stepfathers or another male figure who is not a biological father.

CHAPTER 11

"BROTHER DAVE"

Many young Black fathers don't have the luxury of being as wealthy as professional athletes or entertainers, yet they want to be a part of their children's lives. There are other extenuating circumstances that can prevent fathers from fulfilling their duty as a parent including emotional separation, where tension between parents lead to the father's exclusion from the child's life by the mother.

I have seen instances where animosity between the mother and father of a child is central in the lack of involvement by the father in a child's life. Women who have dissolved the relationship with the father of her child on bad terms may harbor bitterness feeling the need to punish him by keeping the child away.

I read somewhere that NBA players were being told to discard of their own condoms because the women they were sleeping with were bringing the condoms to a medical office and having doctors inseminate them with the sperm left inside the rubber.

Just think about that for a moment. Insane.

After I was able to pick my jaw up from the floor, I wondered what doctor would agree to do something like this. Wasn't the condom used to keep the woman from getting pregnant? I am not a doctor, but I am sure there are some ethics violations here.

With all the coverage given to the irresponsible behavior that leads to accidental pregnancies and the subsequent ridicule of athletes with multiple children by multiple women, the players who take the extra few seconds to protect themselves should not be penalized. It is hard to fathom these guys may have children out there they may be forced to take care of because of opportunistic women and sleazy doctors.

****

What about the fathers that risk their very lives to have a relationship with their child? A close friend I will call "Brother Dave" was living in a Mid-western city with the mother of his son, who I will call Francine. Actually, Brother Dave was allegedly living out of his car, barely eating, wearing the same clothes for three to four days, while Francine was staying with her mother in a nice home.

This was very disturbing to hear to say the least. Brother Dave and Francine met while both were in the Armed Forces. Brother

Dave was deployed to Iraq in 2005. His family spent many a night in prayer circles hoping for his safe return.

These emotional gatherings brought aunts, cousins, and other family that hadn't congregated in weeks together to call on the good Lord to watch over Brother Dave, to cover him, and keep him away from enemy fire. Psalms were sung, Bible verses were read all in an effort to help Brother Dave serve his country safely avoiding the fate of thousands of brave soldiers who will never come home to the families they left behind.

In 2007 the family's prayers were answered as Brother Dave returned with all of his limbs intact and a big surprise: Francine was pregnant. I never met Francine, but my wife had spoken to her over the phone a few times and was not feeling her. Brother Dave and Francine argued a lot and she came across as very controlling and condescending. Francine already had a child as well and the rumor was that she slept around while the two were deployed.

This was all conjecture at this point. In May of 2007 Francine, already living in the Midwest with her family, visited New York for a week and was given a surprise baby shower by Brother Dave's family. I remember Francine, who was almost nine months pregnant at the time, not looking too excited at the gesture of good will.

It was a valiant attempt to get to know her and quell any of the preconceived notions we had about her attitude, but in my opinion she looked very much annoyed and unappreciative of the family's efforts. I understand she may have been in pain or feeling discomfort from her pregnancy, but I don't remember her saying thank you for anything. She rarely spoke at all for that matter.

When his baby was born what should have been happy times for Brother Dave became a nightmare. For the next year and a half, a bunch of horror stories and complaints from Brother Dave finally got me in a car with my wife and his mother for a more than 24-hour road trip.

It was by far the longest I had ever driven. When we finally arrived Brother Dave, anticipating our arrival, came hopping out of the townhouse he was living in by himself. To say it was a sad moment would be an understatement.

Brother Dave was wearing a dusty black hooded sweatshirt, his hair was uncombed and blown out in a lint-filled mini afro, his face was ashy and his mouth looked like he just ate a powdered donut. When he smiled to greet us it was as if his teeth were Pittsburgh Steelers fans: a mix of black and yellow and definitely lacking attention, to put it kindly.

Frankly, he looked homeless. As I greeted Brother Dave I leaned in to give him a pound and I could not stop staring. I had never seen him looking like he did standing before me. He looked like a man that had given up on life, a man content to let the elements take him, resigned to wasting away in a one bedroom flat in front of his Xbox 360.

The sight of Brother Dave in his present condition was too much for his mother to handle. I watched her walk a few feet into the distance. As Brother Dave walked towards the stairs to show us his townhouse, I stayed behind at the car shaking my head. When his mother came back towards me I could see the tears streaming down her face. Her eyes were red and her breaths were deep. She looked up at the sky periodically as if she was asking God how this could happen to her child.

It was a sad scene, but I was glad we made the trip. It was worse than we thought or feared. This was a woman scorned gone bad. Brother Dave wanted nothing but to be in the life of his son and he was paying for that devotion dearly.

Francine's family, mainly her mother, did not like Brother Dave for whatever reason so it was in his best interest to not reside in Francine's home. Without any family here Brother Dave was forced to fend for himself which meant sleeping in his car on many nights.

We weren't sure who was paying for the townhouse he was residing in, but if I remember correctly Brother Dave did have a job. It is possible the money he made at work was paying the rent. Most, if not all, of his income was definitely being funneled to Francine.

The townhouse was a very nice spread. It had clean white carpet throughout the entire place, an eat-in kitchen, and laundry room. The place was completely unfurnished. I looked in the bedroom and saw a single sheet spread across the carpet that served as a bed. The living room was bare save for the Xbox 360 connected to a 9 inch television. Open the refrigerator and it looked like no one lived there. No food, not even survival fare such as eggs, cereal, or the Nissin pack soups that are a lifesaver to college kids. It was heartbreaking. What could he have done to aggravate Francine to the point she would leave him in this condition?

I was heated. 'There was no way I would let this broad do that to me,' I thought. I cursed Francine repeatedly. My profanity filled rant put a smile on Brother Dave's face. While that was not my intent I was glad I could cheer him up somehow.

I realize Brother Dave was only putting himself in this predicament to be close to his son, but he had to draw the line somewhere. This was not right. There is a judicial system that could help make arrangements for child custody or arrange a set amount of child support. It is done all the time with or without the father's consent through garnished wages.

Brother Dave knew his options because his family had been pounding it in his head for months fearing something like this would occur. They warned him about moving so far away specifically because he had no place to go if Francine's family decided to kick him out.

Knowing that Brother Dave had been fairly warned by his family and had the opportunity to settle this predicament in the court system, that we were looking at him in this state made me wonder did he even want a resolution to the issue? For some reason he loved Francine very deeply and maybe he had delusions of them being a happy, harmonious family.

It works both ways. We hear numerous stories of women staying in relationships that are detrimental to their health out of some kind of twisted love or duty to their partner. Sometimes it is for the sake of the children.

Not until you are in that position in that relationship can you judge or tell a person what he or she should do. I know that. It was hard to be objective in this case. I learned that Francine might have been seeing another man all the while leading Brother Dave to believe their relationship still had a chance so she could keep getting money from him. Brother Dave felt he was obligated to provide for his son, but did he know where the money was going?

Brother Dave was definitely being strung along and he was being held hostage by an 18 month-old that looked just like him.

I couldn't blame him. Still I thought how long would he allow himself to be a victim of mental abuse for the sake of his son? It pained me that Brother Dave was giving away all his money and not taking care of himself. He was not eating or bathing, and didn't take any pride in his appearance. He felt he had no alternative and Francine knew this and exploited it.

He would be no good to his kid emaciated and out of his mind. I wanted to tell his family that they can't save someone who doesn't want to be saved. Brother Dave would have to be the one to come to the realization that his relationship with Francine is unhealthy. That he would have to make the decision to walk away or stand up to Francine and not allow her to drain him economically and emotionally.

My logic flew over the head of Brother Dave's mother. She made up her mind she was not coming back to New York without him, child be damned. It would not be that easy. Brother Dave had to get his car back to New York and there were a few loose ends to tie up. It was going to take some time to convince him he needed to be with people who loved and cared for him.

About a month later Brother Dave's mother rented a jeep to take the trip back to the Midwest. This time she was not coming back without her son. It was a 28-hour drive one way and that was driving above the speed limit. Brother Dave's mother was not happy because she would have to take the drive alone with her estranged husband, Brother Dave's father. Their marriage ended badly amidst a web of infidelity, deceit, and lies several years before and this trip would be the first time ex-husband and wife would be in the same space together since about 2002.

Having to drive such a long distance would force the two to speak to each other, if not about unresolved personal issues, about Brother Dave whom they both loved. This was a rescue mission and they would need to put animosity and pride aside for their child.

Ironically it probably was learning the truth about his father's behavior – a fact hidden from Brother Dave for years by his mother to "protect" him – that led to Brother Dave's urgency to remain present in his son's life at all costs.

Two days later they returned with Brother Dave in tow. He drove his car behind his parents all the way back. Even though he was back in New York, Francine still had a hold on him financially. Brother Dave would ultimately get himself together and get a decent job in New York City.

He was still sending money from his personal account to Francine and had not gone to the court to set up a formal arrangement. Although Brother Dave's son spends the majority of his time in another state, he speaks to his son on a daily basis.

Brother Dave is a case where trying to be a devoted father goes terribly wrong when at the mercy of a manipulative woman. He has said many times if not for his son he would have nothing to do with Francine.

While Brother Dave was lucky to return from Iraq in one piece, that is not the case for the thousands of fathers in the military who have lost their lives fighting for our country. This loss can be just as traumatic for children because the parent did not leave on his/her own accord but as a mandatory call of duty. On the other hand the absolute elation and tears of joy on the faces of the children of soldiers who return from their tour of duty is priceless.

The importance of parents in a child's life cannot be overstated. Sometimes it can be taken for granted.

CHAPTER 12

THE GREAT RECESSION

I read a story about a man who mechanically went about his daily routine of going to work in the morning and coming home in the evening to his wife and son. He was the primary bread winner until he got laid off.

He talked about how he felt like less of a man because he wasn't providing monetarily. He was maintaining the household and taking care of his son while his wife worked. He sunk into a deep depression until one day a light bulb went off in his head.

He said all the extra time he was spending with his son he realized he never knew the boy's favorite show was *Yo Gabba Gabba* or his favorite color was blue. He bonded with his son all over again. It dawned on him that during his daily routine he was missing out on precious moments with his child. He realized he was taking his family for granted. It is interesting how a devastating event such as a lay off could be a blessing in disguise.

Working overnights I had plenty of time to spend with Trey during the day. Those who say the years from birth to five years are the best are not lying. I cherished the time I got to watch Trey grow every day. Watching him get taller in size, and develop as a person was a blessing. Witnessing him learn new words, formulate complete sentences and repeat my words or sounds of excitement is hilarious.

It wasn't always easy. There was a time when I questioned if I was being the best father and husband I could be. When I got laid off at the height of the "Great Recession" a few years ago it was a major hindrance in our future plans. Luckily I was only out of work for two months but those 60 days beginning two days before Trey's 2nd birthday was a humbling experience. The pressure was now on my wife to support us which hurt my confidence in my ability as a provider.

I am not one of those guys who has a problem with a woman having a higher salary than a man, I just want to know that I am contributing something. For those two months in 2009 I was embarrassed, even though the layoff had nothing to do with my job performance. My income helped cover costs for sending Trey to school every week, auto insurance payments, utility bills and grocery shopping, among other things.

With unemployment payments barely half of what I was making every week, we had to cut back on the amount of money allotted for these bills which made them pile up. Sometimes payments were missed altogether. We had to dip into our savings for assistance.

A lot of times we as men refuse work because of our foolish pride. Often I have heard things like "I'm not gonna work for 'the man'" or "I wouldn't be caught dead working at McDonalds".

This attitude, especially if you have children, is counterproductive. For one the aforementioned comments will be perceived as copping out or being lazy to the woman in your life who does not want to hear the whining if she is willing to sacrifice her sanity cleaning houses, dealing with overt or covert sexism in the workplace, or babysitting children of wealthy families just to provide for hers.

This is exactly what happened with my father. He wanted the promise of a woman that would take care of him to where he did not have to work. My mom would hear none of it. Why would a man come to a decision like that when small children are part of the equation?

The longer I went without work the more desperate I became. I applied relentlessly to jobs I would never think of doing otherwise like stock person in the supermarket or telephone salesperson for a cable company (nothing against those jobs, but I was overqualified and had no experience respectively which is probably why I did not receive a call for an interview).

I felt like I was failing my family. I thought about my writing career and why it had not taken off. I thought about all the screenplays I had written and procrastinated on re-writing, not fully taking advantage of my headshots, or going to the free acting classes when I was getting a lot of work as an extra in commercials and music videos. I thought about my music career, how my self-criticism of my mix tapes kept me from pounding the pavement and promoting it even though I was repeatedly told how good it was.

I could not help but think I should have been making money in my field. I was holding myself back. I was being complacent, not happy that I was not making any money in writing yet not angry enough to really push myself to make it happen. Creating a small buzz and then stalling was not cutting it. Finishing a screenplay, entering it in a competition and making the quarterfinal round should not have been acceptable. Yet it was.

I felt like I was a bad father. My salary should have been equal to Tracy-Ann's and we should have been in our dream home with Trey able to run around in a backyard, in his own room where his millions of toys could breathe in their own little paradise. I should only have been waking up to walk to my laptop to write the next story, scene, or lyric from the comfort of my home.

Instead I was perusing the bootleg classified sections of newspapers, uploading my resume on job sites where only no frills temp agencies post openings. This was not how life was supposed to be for us.

I was wasting time and because of that I had nothing to fall back on once the job that kept me afloat let the air out of my life boat. It was a horrible feeling. I suddenly knew how that guy that got reacquainted with his son after his layoff felt, yet I did not have to get to know my son. I just wanted him to be happy, and he was because he could not understand the severity of this crisis. All he knew was daddy was home all day and every day.

Still having to see my wife's grandmother not see me go to work, not see me provide was killing me inside. I felt the emptiness, the insecurity, the struggle, wondering if this would be the straw that breaks the marriage. My wife understood a layoff is out of my control, but that did not mean she was not worried about what was going to happen next.

I really beat myself up over the course of the two months I was out of work. I guess the fact that I wasn't nonchalant about being unemployed, like my father was so many years before, counted for something. Instead of getting up and walking away from my family because of what I could not do for them financially, I realized that just being there and providing love and doing my job as a husband and father was just as important.

Trey did not care that I did not have money on a certain day to pay a bill, he was just happy I was home. Still there were times that I wish I had more financially to give Trey all that he deserved. Being woken up by his voice saying "daddy" or seeing his infectious smile or hearing his wild hearty laugh when he is amused by his own internal joke gives me the strength to push forward with my writing in anticipation of a breakthrough. The faith and support of my wife, her determination, her tough love when I am derailed by procrastination or some other distraction, solidifies my drive to make a better way for us.

****

My wife surprised me for Valentine's Day 2011 with a copy of Jay-Z's book *Decoded*. Being a fan of Hip Hop music and lyricism she knew I would love to read the book. More than the book itself, the message she wrote on the inside cover was extremely touching.

Without going into her exact words, she reminded me that she believed I would fulfill my goals. She said she knows I will be the man that God made for her. I definitely was not reaching my potential at the time and most women would probably leave a guy whose lofty dreams of a comfortable life were all lip service to that point.

There were times before we were married when I was living paycheck to paycheck. Although Tracy-Ann never came off as someone who was materialistic, like any woman she loved to shop and desired the finest things. It was difficult for me to buy her what she wanted all the time. She made her way through college earning her Bachelor's and Master's degree in Psychology and Social Work respectively and was fortunate enough to work her way up the ranks from a Social Worker traveling to different houses throughout the five boroughs, to Program Coordinator and Director in her field.

She had the means to buy her own things, which did not always make me feel the best. I would tell her she did not deserve someone like me who could not give her the finest material things. I was looking for an easy way out of the relationship without admitting my insecurities outright.

Each time I made this stupid comment my future wife shut me down. She told me the same thing: she did not care about what I could buy her, she just wanted me to get myself together. She wanted me to reach my creative potential because that would make me happy. If I was happy I would do more to make sure she had everything she wanted emotionally and physically.

Whenever you have a woman that refuses to give up on you when you are unwittingly doing all you can to mess things up, it is best to keep her at all costs.

Her words let me know she will always have my back and that is all you can ask from the love of your life. How can I walk away from the two people that love me that much for being myself?

Why do you think most celebrities end up with either the person they were with before they were famous or the person that did not fall all over them? LL Cool J's wife Simone paid him no attention at a time when he was arguably the biggest rap star in music and everyone knew who he was. She was dead serious in her ignorance.

It's hard to find true love in a position of power and LL knew he had a winner and eventually did the right thing by her.

My wife has always told me she fears when I become successful that I will leave her for a more affluent lifestyle. My father wasn't rich when he left, quite the opposite. With that as my back story I have to believe I would use any God-given wealth to uplift my family. Anything less would make me a hypocrite.

Sure there is a lot of pressure on celebrities and temptations come from all sides. All I have to do is look at Grant Hill and Boris Kodjoe and see these men at the height of their respective fields, traveling constantly away from their significant others, but still keep the fire burning in their marriage. The love in their eyes when around their wives is still present. No amount of money can buy or replace that. More importantly their kids see the strength of two loving parents through unimaginable social pressure and scrutiny.

I named my first laptop "Trey Amani's Future" because I felt his future depended on my success as a writer. It is a big expectation to put on myself especially in a field that is not easy to break into.

But that is what a father does. He takes on the burden, shields his child from the ugliness, the hate, the crabs-in-a-barrel mentality, the racism, and the skepticism of the outside world. He keeps his child in that cartoon world of laughter and happily ever after endings for as long as humanly possible. Even when the child reaches the phallic stage a father is there to answer all questions, deflect all slings and arrows, rationalize negativity and other adult issues levied at the child through an unforgiving social media.

The birds and the bees, playing team sports, learning to drive: everything my father missed out on teaching me I want to teach my son. The quality time is priceless, but the stability of a regular income is just as important.

CHAPTER 13

HIP HOP FATHERS

Many of Hip Hop's superstars regularly convey the pain of their own fatherless childhood on record. Legendary rapper LL Cool J, a devoted father of four, wrote in his 1997 autobiography _"I Make My Own Rules"_ about the abuse he suffered at the hands of his stepfather and released a touching ode to the biological father who failed to live up to his title on 1997's _"Father"_ off his album _Phenomenon_. The chorus simply stated _"all I ever wanted/ all I ever needed was a father...that's all."_ (_see Appendix i._)

"Having a child shouldn't have to bring out the man in me/ plus I wanted you to be raised in a family/ I don't wanna, go through the drama of having a baby's momma/ weekend visits and buyin J's ain't gon' make me a father" (Common. _"Retrospect For Life"_ from the album _One Day It Will All Make Sense_, 1997) [_see Appendix i._]

There are many notable Hip Hop artists who are fathers; artists that are ridiculed and attacked by the mainstream media like _Common,_ called a "thug" by Republicans when he was invited to recite poetry at the White House (anyone who has heard *Common's* music knows that is ridiculous), *Big Boi* of *Outkast*, and *T.I.* regularly step up and take care of their children, even mentioning their kids in their lyrics. These are men who went through turbulent childhoods and are determined not to make the same mistakes with their own seeds.

The aforementioned *LL Cool J* put his eldest son in the music video for his 2004 single *"Hush"* as a younger version of himself, showing the effort to be a parent who spends time with his children despite the hectic schedule that comes with being an international superstar.

Common teamed up with rapper/singer/actress *Lauryn Hill* in 1997 for a touching ode to parenthood called *"Retrospect for Life"* off of his third album *One Day It'll All Make Sense*, a song where *Common* struggles with the decision of terminating an unwanted pregnancy due to his lack of maturity. After walking out on his girlfriend and four and a half minutes of soul-searching, *Common* decides he is ready to raise a child and returns to support the mother of his unborn. This song shows even though he did not want the pregnancy the child still deserves a chance to live.

Most notable devoted fathers are Diddy, Snoop Dogg, and 50 Cent. All three of these men have been lambasted in the media for irresponsible behavior or lyrical content. Although these three are not the best role models in terms of their lifestyle (Snoop has promoted porn videos, 50's lyrics are flooded with violent references, Diddy is notorious for hard partying), there is no question that they love their children.

Diddy, whose father was murdered when he was just three years old, always finds time for his kids, placing his two oldest biological sons Justin and Christian in ads for his clothing line *Sean John* coined after Combs' real first and middle name. He is a step-father to his ex-girlfriend - and mother of three of his children including the aforementioned Christian and twin girls D'lila Star & Jesse James - Kim's oldest son Quincy, and he acknowledged a daughter named Chance he fathered while with Kim after taking a DNA test in 2007.

50 Cent went to a judge to set an amount for monthly child support payments because he felt the mother of his son Marquise was taking advantage of his considerable wealth by requesting exorbitant monthly payments. Although 50 and his son have recently become estranged for reasons known only to them, the effort to be a visible presence is evident. These three entertainers live their lives in the public eye and under tremendous scrutiny, yet realize the welfare of their children is a top priority.

Snoop Dogg (who was the poster child for the criticism of misogyny on wax when his *Doggystyle* album dropped in 1993) had a hit television show that chronicled the life of his real family on the E! television network. Like Ice Cube, Snoop has transcended his controversial past appearing in commercials with billionaire Warren

Buffet among other unlikely appearances. He is also giving back to his community while being a social father figure to a number of kids in his Snoop Youth Football League.

50's mother was murdered when he was a pre-teen and he never knew his father. He had to grow up quick and he chose dealing drugs as a way to make ends meet. 50, who recently became a father for the second time, is one of the biggest names in entertainment and he has not let his past interfere with how he raises his youngest son. It is further evidence of how having a child changes your perspective on life, even the hardest of rappers.

It is important to remember that these guys are human beings. They have real government names like ordinary civilians. Although their stage persona and image is over-the-top, it is just entertainment for the purpose of selling their brand. It is their job to be creative.

I think a lot of the critics of Hip Hop music and its artists lose sight of the human element. Most times the behavior of the artists draw the negative coverage by overtly bragging about their pasts as drug dealers, promoting the pimp lifestyle, and partying harder than the average person. These guys have faced real life consequences for their actions and affiliations. Snoop Dogg fought for his freedom in 1993 while on trial for the murder of a rival gang member, 50 was infamously shot nine times, and Puffy had to deal with being fired from his executive position at Uptown records, then the death of his flagship Bad Boy recording artist Notorious B.I.G. in 1997 and allegations that he fired a gun in a club in 1999, a case that went to trial.

It is true a lot of young people are heavily influenced by what their favorite rappers say is cool and how they wear their clothing, but it goes back to the idea of who should be role models to the youth. Think about it, a lot of rappers may talk tough in their lyrics, but the last place they want to be is in jail or worse.

Over time the line between reporting on violence in the Black community and glorifying it became blurred. I firmly support the artists who reported on the horrors of their condition because otherwise the injustice would continue to occur.

It is not a coincidence that many rappers throughout the history of Hip Hop came out of situations of privation and poverty. For most of these rappers poverty, drugs, crime, and broken homes are all they knew growing up.

That they were able to put their feelings into words that happen to rhyme is an enormously difficult skill. It was called poetry the last time I checked. If the rap artists were not going through the issues they spoke about, they knew someone that was in jail, that got killed in a drive-by shooting, or pulled over by police for driving while Black.

A lot of these artists were kids when they came into the spotlight so many years ago and now they have kids of their own. The overwhelming thought with not just entertainers but fathers in general is that their kids will not go through the same hardships. This is why you saw lavish sweet sixteen parties for Justin Combs for example. Christian Combs dancing alongside his dad on stage.

These kids are privileged to get the finest of everything and, even though it may seem over-the-top to the modern day everyman, the Hip Hop fathers are only passing on the rewards of their hard work and dedication, their blood sweat and tears. These kids saw their father's hard work first hand watching them constantly travel from city to city to keep their brand relevant and income flowing in. One can only hope these kids take with them the lessons of hard work that have afforded them the extravagant lifestyle they are living.

Trey's closet was full of Air Jordans and the best name brand clothes we could buy from the time he was born. Do you know what I was wearing as a kid? The finest in Zips and Kangaroos footwear. Times have definitely changed and I make no apologies for my Le Tigre and Osh Kosh B'gosh shirts.

It is still ironic to me that the relatively fun, party style Hip Hop music of the '80s never really exploded onto the mainstream, but as soon as rappers began talking about shooting people, selling drugs, calling women out of their name, and all the negative images relative to the degradation of African-American men and women, the music began to sell to a crossover audience.

It was also at this point that critics started voicing their displeasure, but it was their sons and daughters who were making these artists rich by purchasing the music and emulating what they heard and saw in the videos. Why shouldn't these rappers who suffered through horrible conditions reap the benefits of mainstream exposure, especially when they have their own families to support?

It is just my thoughts ladies and gentlemen.

CHAPTER 14

HE GOT GAME

Incarceration is a huge factor in the separation of fathers in the African American community from their children. The men's rights activist Glenn Sacks regularly publicizes situations in which government authorities target so-called "deadbeat" parents, noting that jailing people for non-payment can be ineffective if the parent is identified incorrectly as neglectful.

According to the article *Parental Imprisonment, the Prison Boom, and the Concentration of Childhood Disadvantage* "1 in 40 White children born in 1978 and 1 in 25 White children born in 1990 had a parent imprisoned" while "1 in 7 Black children born in 1978 and 1 in 4 Black children born in 1990 had a parent imprisoned." (Wildeman p.267)

The disproportionate amount of African American males in the penal system is glaring in itself, but even in dire circumstances, there are incarcerated men who are working hard to educate themselves on how to be a father once they return to society.

I work with adolescent inmates currently residing at Rikers Island jail facility. They are 16 and 17 years of age and many of them have pictures in their cell of newborn babies. It is hard to fathom these kids having babies of their own, not only because they cannot take care of them because they are behind bars, but the responsibility of a new mouth to feed outside of jail does not alter their deviant behavior one bit on the inside.

I have talked about how Trey's birth changed my outlook on life, but with these kids it seems to have no effect on their mentality whatsoever. I would like to believe it is a front for other inmates. The fact of the matter is these kids have to portray a hardcore persona just to survive being bullied, extorted or assaulted. It is a sad existence. Many of the inmates know each other from their respective neighborhoods, friends and enemies alike, and they are all in gangs.

I have been on the job long enough to see the human side of many of these so-called thugs. Whether I am in earshot of their phone calls to loved ones or during a quiet moment when everyone is locked in, these youths do let their guard down and show some vulnerability. Jail is no place I wanted to be at 16 and I made sure whenever I was part of a group headed for trouble I made myself scarce. I immediately thought about how upset my mom would be if I was ever arrested or not wanting to let my grandmothers down. Many of these young men don't think about the repercussions of their behavior until after they have been caught. There are some that are career criminals who constantly leave the Island just to return days or weeks later and think it is a badge of honor, but there are a few that don't belong at Rikers at all.

I was working on the visit floor and saw a kid walk out to see an older lady (probably his mother), and a young girl (maybe his sister), and collapse at their feet in tears. I witnessed an inmate walk out to his mother who was waiting in the visit chair only for her to start sobbing uncontrollably. I can only imagine what these parents are going through. It has to be heartbreaking to see your child locked up.

I try to pull these future leaders aside and let them know whatever they did or continue to do that landed them in jail must cease. Especially if they are fathers, I make sure I let them know their child depends on them being visible and alive to teach them the right way. The way I see it if I can get through to one of these kids I have done my job.

****

He Got Game (*Directed by Spike Lee, 1998*) is a striking testament to the father/son bond shared through the game of basketball. Jake Shuttlesworth, played by Denzel Washington, accidentally kills his wife which ultimately gets him arrested and removed from his children, but uses the love of basketball he shares with his son to return to his life.

This is another one of my favorite films - directed by one of my influences as a screenwriter: *Spike Lee* - because I am a die-hard sports fan and I had not seen the issue of fatherhood tackled in this manner on screen. Jake has to deal with the resentment of his son Jesus Shuttlesworth (played by NBA superstar Ray Allen). During Jake's time away, Jesus assumes the role of mother and father to his younger sister Mary.

Jesus took on the added responsibility at a time when he was under intense scrutiny and pressure being touted as the best high school player in the country. Shuttlesworth embraced the role of guardian, admirable since he easily could have adopted a negative attitude in light of his situation and taken his anger out on Mary.

In reality some media journalists would likely dismiss Jake as a violent convict completely missing the bigger picture: Jake's arrest removed him from his children. Where too many young Black men are placed in a position of breadwinner or "man of the house" at a young age, few have a male mentor to help relieve the stress. Jake knew that the best thing he could do for his son was remain visible in his life.

What made Jake powerful was that he did not allow himself to become a statistic in prison. He worked out an arrangement where he could receive an early release from prison if he could convince Jesus to go to the warden's alma mater, the fictional Ball State.

Jake fought to keep in contact with his children, attempting to reconnect with Jesus, who was still bitter over the death of his mother. Jesus treats Jake as a "deadbeat dad" referring to Jake by his first name, similar to Will's character in *Fresh Prince*. However, Jake never quit on his children.

Before his jail time, Jake bonded with Jesus through basketball, teaching Jesus everything he knows in flashback scenes of physical one on one competition similar to Kyrie Irving and his father. The image of the father/son relationship is positive at this point as Jake is fostering the physical and emotional growth of Jesus passing the torch of a sport Jake played on to his son.

The climax of the movie is a one on one game between Jesus and Jake to decide where Jesus goes to school. The stakes are high as Jake offers to stay out of Jesus' life if his son wins, but if Jake wins, Jesus has to attend Ball State.

Jesus wins the contest, gaining redemption (by knocking his father to the floor while scoring the winning basket) from the days of his youth where Jake won all the games. Jesus quickly dismisses Jake. Jake, crushed that his son is so cold to him, responds "get that hate out your heart, boy." Jesus ultimately goes to Ball state showing that Jake did make an impact with his presence.

My analysis of this scene is that Jesus never really wanted Jake out of his life. The game was a way to fully take out his anger on the loss of his mother on Jake. Jesus was finally able to inflict the same physical on-court punishment to his father that he endured as a child. Again, closure is achieved.

Although Jake stands to gain an early release from jail by convincing his son to go to a specific college, it is apparent that regaining the love and trust of Jesus was more important than his personal gain. This reiterates the act of putting the child before the father, a key character element that encourages the growth of the father-son relationship.

Using sports, in this case basketball, to highlight the importance of the father-son dynamic is genius in my opinion. *He Got Game* had so many similarities to my life in terms of the way Jesus felt about his father once Jake reappeared in his life. Ray Allen had no acting experience before that film, and was probably cast in the film because of his ability as a basketball player, but what may have started out as a goal to have authentic basketball scenes turned into a heartfelt portrayal of a child betrayed.

I felt Jesus' hurt towards Jake for killing his mom and effectively removing himself from the family by going to jail. I felt the disgust for Jake as Jesus knocked him to the floor in the aforementioned one-on-one basketball game. I watched Ray Allen in that movie and thought that would probably be how I would react to my own father if I had seen him on the street. It was equally important that Jake stood up to Jesus and effectively told him enough was enough re-establishing his authority. Although Jesus did not respect Jake at the time he had to recognize that his father did not give up on him and their relationship.

I would have liked to see my father pull me aside and tell me his side of the story. Tell me he had enough of me thinking he was a horrible person. It is never too late to make amends with children left behind. I believe absentee fathers owe their children that opportunity for closure. I was still running away from seeing my father, but God works in mysterious ways.

Something had to give.

CHAPTER 15

REUNION

My father's mother died on the morning of my 30th birthday: September 1st 2008. What was great about my grandmother, besides the fact that she put me on to how great graham crackers tasted, she was so full of love. She consistently reminded my father how dumb (probably not the word she used) he was to leave my mom, my sister, and I.

Each and every time she saw my mother she brought up my father, like my mom was gonna jump up and ask "where is he?" There was not going to be a fairytale ending. My mom had moved on long ago. My grandmother was an eternal optimist, an elderly Chuck Woolery[8] if you will.

The last time I saw my grandmother alive was in 2004 in Tampa, Florida. My family was in town to celebrate her sister-in-law's 75th birthday. My grandmother, at an advanced age, made her

---

[8] Chuck Woolery was the host of the matchmaking television game show "Love Connection" which aired from 1983-1994

bed in a nursing home. Having long lost the ability to walk on her own power, she still had her mental faculties.

Her room was as bland as a nursing home room is expected to be. White walls, spotted white floors, and drab drapery hung from a curtain rod. A closer look, however, and you would find my grandmother's stamp throughout the room.

There were picture frames of family members on the small drawers positioned on each side of the bed. As she sat in the loveseat next to her bed, her favorite stuffed animal rested on the newly made up mattress.

Our appearance was a welcome surprise as my grandmother was very unhappy living in the nursing home. What hurt her more was that she could not be near her family. A woman who never forgot a birthday, always had a birthday or Christmas card for family members and friends alike (not to mention money in my birthday cards), was incapacitated; a prisoner of her own inability to move around. She couldn't live in her own home, couldn't go to church or see family and friends at her leisure and it saddened her immensely.

On numerous occasions I would hear that she would cry asking for her family. She wanted to come back to New York where she had lived in Brooklyn on Troy Ave between Foster Avenue and Farragut Road for so many years. It broke my heart no one would take her out of the nursing home. The cold hard fact was everyone had their own responsibilities. No one had time to give round the clock care to my grandmother in her condition.

The nurses I met at the nursing home that day were very pleasant. I didn't get the sense that my grandmother was being abused or neglected as is often the case with the elderly in these situations. And the nurses could not put up a front for the family around my grandmother. She would blow up their spot quickly. She didn't say a bad word about any of the nurses we met. That gave me some solace.

I quickly realized my grandmother had not changed a bit. She was still the biggest cheerleader in my mother and father's fan club. Ever since he left the family she had been apologizing for his behavior as if she was reading a prepared statement. My mother usually laughed this off. At the nursing home, sure enough, as soon as we walked in the door and pleasantries were exchanged she let it be known my father was in town as well.

As you might have guessed, that signature nervous feeling ran through my stomach. There was no more ducking in the park. No hiding around the corner until he left my aunt's house. I was definitely going to be in the same room with my father for the first time since Ronald Reagan was President of the United States.

I think I was ready to see him now. I had given up on the fire and brimstone feelings of angst. I mean, I had no choice. I couldn't stay in the hotel. There was a lot of other family I had not seen in years.

This party was like a reunion of my father's side and I wasn't about to let the fear of seeing him stop me from attending.

The evening of the party I was looking forward to greeting a lot of my cousins, aunts and uncles I hadn't seen in over 15 years when we were all pre-teens.

The hall where the party was being kept was festive. Balloons, streamers, and signs that read "Happy Birthday" were hung all around the room. There was a huge chair fit for a queen near the main table reserved for my grand aunt.

As I exchanged pleasantries with relatives, everyone looked practically as I remembered. I would love to say that I was giving everyone my undivided attention, but I would be bending the truth a little. I knew my father was in the room somewhere like an 800 pound gorilla.

As the night went on I searched the room for my father and probably passed over him many times. I was looking for his trademark beard. Someone in the room pointed him out to me. When I saw him I rose to my feet. The moment I had waited two years of my young life for, then avoided for the past decade and a half was finally here. As I walked over to him he stood up when he saw me. It seemed like he knew who I was or maybe somebody told him. I think someone tipped him off that it was me because my physical features obviously changed over 15 years. His changed too.

He was clean shaven. The only time I saw my father without a beard was in old photos taken in the early 1970s way before I was thought of. I looked at those pictures from time to time. There were pictures of my mother and my father in vintage '70s wardrobe: platform shoes, bellbottom pants, tight-fitting button down shirt, and my father rocking the Elvis Presley sideburns. They married in 1974 and the date on this photo said the year was 1973.

Surprisingly I was not nervous. As I strode over to meet my father it was like I was meeting a stranger, someone I was supposed to remember from my youth but couldn't. He was two tables away but it felt like I was walking forever. It was like a movie scene where the action stops around us and I am in slow motion. I felt no animosity just a need to get past the moment.

I extended my right hand and my father extended his. It was a firm shake that led to an embrace. I can't say the hug stirred anything inside of me. I took a moment to look at him. It was weird that I was now taller than he was. His hair was cut very low almost clean shaven as well. This was a visage I was not used to. It took a moment for my brain to process the image I was seeing, like walking out of a very dark room into sunlight.

I did glance down at his left hand and saw a wedding band on his ring finger. He had remarried. That was his right. My mother did.

He introduced me to the people at the table where he was sitting. There were two guys and a girl. He said their names, or maybe he didn't. It was all a blur. As I shook the hands of these people a million thoughts ran through my head. The guys looked like they were my age.

'Were any of these people related to me?' was one thought.

'Did I have another brother or sister?' was another.

I never gave serious thought to the possibility the woman my father left us for may have had a child for him. He was only in his mid-thirties at the time. Come to think of it, I never saw the woman at all. I'm sure she wasn't there. However, the ultimate slap-in-the-face to an abandoned child was possibly staring at me with three sets of eyes. I was cordial.

What was I going to say: 'Hi, are you my brother?'

None of my thoughts were confirmed that night so these must have been the people he left me and my mom to inherit. As they smiled at me I smiled back shaking their hands. I knew these were people I would never see again after this moment, so why commit them to memory? Amazingly I wasn't angry. My calmness scared me.

Maybe if the setting was different I would have had a different reaction, but for some reason even though I never looked over my shoulder or around the room it felt like the whole place was watching me to see what I would do around my father or, worse yet, to him.

It was like people were waiting to see one of those stop the music moments in entertainment where the sound of a punch interrupts the party scene followed by the scream of a shocked female. Or maybe they were expecting me to crumble in a slobbering mass at his feet overcome with the emotion such a reunion would bring. I was much too classy for that, brought up by a mother that chose never to embarrass me with a public beating.

"Let me talk to you for a minute, son".

And with that my father and I walked away from his table to an isolated area yards away. It was coming. The obligatory apology followed by the excuse.

"It's good to see you, son."

"It's good to see you," I said.

My answers were short.

I cut to the chase. I didn't wait all these years to exchange pleasantries. I remember asking why he left us behind.

"I'm sorry about that son, but I had my hands tied," my father explained.

"It was either leave or stay and something terrible happen."

As a ten year-old I waited for my father to walk back through the door. As an 11 year-old I still held out hope. When my mother and I moved to Chester Court I hoped my father would ask my aunt to reach out to my mother so he could get our new address and come back. I waited years for an answer, for some kind of clarity and I was left with the total opposite.

That was the big explanation?

Are you kidding me?

I didn't respond. I just nodded my head. For the life of me I could not speak. I think I was stunned by the excuse. His hands were tied? I could have asked him why he felt his hands were tied or what were the terrible things that could have happened if he stayed.

I could have definitely brought up the alleged job he had off the books so the courts couldn't garnish his wages for child support, but for some reason I did not feel like having an extended conversation. Maybe he thought the reason was good enough.

It wasn't.

I thought he was the same old liar that acted like everything was okay over the phone that July evening years ago. He lied then, he lied when he said he wasn't leaving that morning in the living room.

If he had a side to his story that would refute what my mother told me, the arguments I witnessed due to his coming home late at night, and the aforementioned falsehoods, this would be the time to share it.

My subdued reaction was all the proof I needed that the emotional attachment was gone. Either that or I had finally let the anger of that little boy go way before this reunion. Or maybe I just knew what to expect and got exactly what I thought. After a few minutes we both went back to our tables.

Some may ask why after 15 years I would still want answers from my father about his sudden departure. Why did Jay-Z want answers from his father after they reunited some 20 odd years after leaving his household? Confronting the person you looked up to as a youngster and getting answers about the traumatizing event brings closure to the situation.

I didn't get an explanation for the abandonment when it happened, not even a year, not even five, ten, or fifteen years after. My wife says I was stuck in the body of that little kid that was left behind and she was absolutely right. It was like my world stopped. I finally got to face my father, look him in the eye and get his story. I definitely let him off the hook by not asking the tough questions.

Why didn't I ask? I envisioned another time and place for the heart to heart, but would I even see him again after tonight? He took my number, but he had my number back then too. I took his number as well, but it didn't feel genuine. It was like taking a number from an old friend you hadn't seen in years. More than likely you have no intention of calling and the person that gave you the number isn't really expecting a call.

I didn't speak to my father the rest of that evening until it was time to leave the party, but word got back to me that he was telling people if he died that day he would be a happy man because he saw me.

Give me a break. How cliché was that comment? As if a validation of my detached feelings that night, of course my father's chorus of joy would revert back to the same old song over the next few years.

● ●

CHAPTER 16

FUNERAL

On the night of August 31st 2008, Trey would not stop crying. The waterworks came suddenly. My wife and I struggled to figure out what was wrong. We thought over what he had eaten the entire day. Was it sour milk? He was only a year and a half old, so any unexplainable events meant a trip to the hospital. My wife was that cautious. I didn't blame her. It was a trying pregnancy and "nine months of torture", as she so eloquently put it, meant not taking any chances.

I was more of the mindset of saving a trip to the emergency room unless it was extremely necessary.

For me, Trey had to be in grave danger: throwing up repeatedly where it is just water after a while, hitting his head extremely hard where he doesn't stop crying, or he had an extremely high fever that wouldn't break.

I wanted to avoid hospital bills if it was something we could take care of. Besides, one of our closets looked like an emergency room with the amount of remedies we had for Trey. There was a bottle of nasal drops, a bottle for gas pain, Tylenol, suppositories, Benadryl, Q-tips, you name it.

I convinced Tracy-Ann to ride it out. After about a half an hour Trey stopped crying and fell back asleep. He slept the rest of the night.

The next morning I got a call from my mother telling me my grandmother had died. I couldn't believe it. I saw the condition she was in four years earlier. I knew she was getting older, we all are, but you still don't expect to get the phone call.

I think we all expect our family members to live forever, especially if they are not suffering from any major diseases. When God decides it is your time to be with Him, it is that time. We are on His watch.

It doesn't make it any easier to take. I would be going back to Florida. Tracy-Ann and I decided to leave Trey in New York mainly because we did not want him to see death up close like that. He could misinterpret the motionless body with the eyes closed for sleep. This was a permanent nap and we did not want to possibly traumatize him with that image.

Heading back to Florida meant seeing my father again. Our reunion four years earlier had not yielded any more instances of father-son bonding. After returning to New York that year we pretty much went back to our respective lives: me back to Brooklyn and him back into the witness protection program.

He was invited to attend my wedding just a year later in 2005 and he refused allegedly claiming he needed surgery on his foot. His two brothers told a different story in Jamaica during a bonding session days before the nuptials.

My uncles told me they offered to pay his plane ticket and room at the Half Moon resort in Montego Bay just so he could not make the excuse that he didn't have any money. Hearing this took me back to when I was a little boy. It felt like he was going out of his way to avoid me for some reason. He had no obligation to come around, but my uncles along with everyone else believed he should have been present for the biggest day 'of my life at that point. I especially thought it would be fitting that he show up seeing that we supposedly got the awkwardness of the reunion out of the way.

It is not like that would have been the first time we were seeing each other since 1989. I was disappointed. I felt this man should have hopped on to a plane with one leg to be there for his son. I think he owed me that much.

I wanted to trust my father again, or at least begin to. In my opinion if someone is offering you an all expense paid trip to the Caribbean and you get a chance to attend a special occasion involving your son virtually for free and you refuse something is very wrong with you.

I'm not going to lie I was more than disappointed. My father's absence from my wedding under those circumstances pissed me off. It was like back to square one. I gave him another opening to try to repair our relationship, but it was like someone hit reverse on the conveyor belt.

Once again I was that disappointed little boy. That after 16 years and one weak excuse he had the audacity not to show up for the most important day of my life, I believed he did not really want to reconcile. Maybe the handshake and hug a year earlier was just for show. Maybe he felt he had to put on a good face for everyone in the room.

Could he be that callous? I gave him the benefit of the doubt. Maybe he was so guilt-ridden that he couldn't bring himself to come to the wedding, especially since the father plays a major role in the proceedings. Maybe he did not want to be around my family members who would likely ask him some very tough questions about me or, worse yet, ridicule him from afar.

It didn't matter. If God spares my life I would never miss a major event like Trey's wedding.

****

Viewing my grandmother's body was not as difficult as I thought it would be. I walked into the funeral home and greeted a few of my family members who were already there.

From the back of the parlor I could see a white coffin surrounded by floral arrangements. The room was small enough where I could make out my grandmother's head sticking up from out of the coffin. To the right of her coffin there was a poster board on an easel with her picture and her entry and exit dates from the realm of the living written along the bottom.

To the left of her coffin I saw my uncle Cliff, the oldest child, sitting in the front row looking straight at his mother's body. He wasn't crying, just in his own world. It felt as if he thought his mother's body would miraculously move if he stared at it long and hard enough. That's a symptom of disbelief I suppose.

My father stood to his left in a white button down shirt. He was facing the coffin just above his mother's head. I could see that he was very emotional. He kept burying his face in the tissue he was holding, rubbing his eyes with the backside of his right hand.

I got the sense he was not only crying for the current state of his mother, but the guilt over the numerous times she begged him to visit her and he did not, the numerous promises he made to her that he would show up and he did not, promises that were all too familiar to me.

Conversely my Uncle Donovan, the youngest of my grandmother's five kids had made frequent trips to Florida to see his mother. It seemed like every other week I heard that Uncle "Donny" was either in Florida or headed to the Sunshine State. Four of my grandmother's children were in Florida for her funeral and my Uncle Donny was the only one I did not see break down the entire time.

It would seem that he treated her best in her final years since he basically made sure she was taken care of. He had a clear conscience in terms of making peace with his mother. The others, I wasn't so sure. Seeing my father was a blubbering mass of flesh told me that he genuinely missed his mother and he was coming to grips with the reality of her passing.

Life is too short. My grandmother did not ask for much, just to be near her family. I said as much as I gave her eulogy the next day at the church she attended every Sunday until she was unable to physically appear anymore.

It was decided after the viewing that I would do the honors. My Uncle Donny was going to do it by default, but my sister nominated me. I had never given a eulogy before, but I didn't hesitate to accept the honor. I spent the rest of the evening in the hotel organizing my thoughts on the notepad provided in the room. I had an idea what I would say. I would just let everyone know what my grandmother meant to me.

Not surprisingly the church was packed for my grandmother's funeral service. Family and friends from all walks of her life filled the room. The last five rows on the right side facing out from the stage were filled with friends and patients from the nursing home where she lived the last five years. They were the only White people in the room. It was touching to see. She touched a lot of lives in her time on Earth.

I was seated near the rear of the church on the left side next to Tracy-Ann, my mother and my sister. When it was time to read the eulogy my uncle began to rise as if by instinct, then he looked back at me. I stood up and took the long walk to the stage passing the closed casket on my way up the steps.

When I reached the podium I reached in my pocket and pulled out the crumpled yellow sheet of paper that had the rough draft of my eulogy. I hadn't bothered to rewrite it because I knew all I needed was a reference point and I could go from there. I shouldn't have to read completely from a paper if I was speaking from the heart.

I looked down at the paper once and looked up at the throng of people in front of me. It wasn't the first time I had all eyes on me on a stage. You would think performing Hip Hop shows across the United States in cities like New York, St. Louis, Washington D.C., Baltimore and Stone Mountain, Georgia in front of strangers, standing in front of family members would be nothing for me. Not the case. I still felt the nervousness in the pit of my stomach the same as when I was getting ready to perform. During a show the nervous energy would dissipate once the music started. I would lose myself in the track and become a different person according to my wife and others who have seen me in action.

There would be no music serving as a backdrop to this eulogy. There would be no moving around the stage evading the watchful gaze of a fickle crowd. I had to stand in one place and give a speech.

Standing still and speaking to an audience is totally different than performing. There was nowhere to hide in that solitary position at the podium. I had to look my audience directly in the eye to be effective whereas at a Hip Hop show the stage lighting would blind my sight more times than not and I could give the impression that I was looking at the crowd without seeing them directly.

Luckily I recognized a lot of the faces in the audience. I saw family in my cousin Sherry that I had not seen in five years. Sherry is my Uncle Cliff's daughter. She was very emotional at the viewing. I looked behind her and saw my father. His head was up but his eyes were looking down at the pew in front of him.

He could not look at me.

I looked to his left and saw my cousin Andre and his sister. Everyone looked somber. Speaking from the heart I ran through all my memories of my grandmother: how she got me hooked on graham crackers and her inimitable laugh, which I decided to do an impression of. This drew laughter from the entire room because it was spot-on. My grandmother laughed a lot so everyone in the church was immediately drawn to a memory of her signature chortle.

I told the story of Trey crying uncontrollably the night before my birthday. I spoke about how everyone needed to be happy that my grandmother lived a full life. I noted that she would not want everyone to be crying over her. I looked back at my father and he was still looking down, but he was smiling.

I told the room that my grandmother loved her family. All she wanted was to be near the people she loved and took care of as she got older.

I ended the eulogy by thanking everyone who knew and loved her for their support. Then I asked for God to bless her and watch over her. I remember ending the eulogy by saying "grandma". I walked off the stage, walked up to the casket, put my lips to my left hand and touched the casket with the same hand before walking the long mile it seemed down the aisle back to my seat.

The silence in the church was a little awkward. I didn't know what I expected at that moment. Applause? No. I just expected someone to say something as I walked back. My Uncle Barry extended his hand and nodded his head as he mouthed the words "good job."

One person that was missing from the service was my cousin Oliver. He was my grandmother's first grandchild. When I visited her house in New York, color photos of Oliver as a pre-teen adorned her dresser. Their birthdays fell in the same month of December.

Oliver was missing in action because he was driving to Florida from New York!

When he finally arrived at the cemetery with his family he was a ball of emotion. He hugged my father and started crying immediately before even reaching her casket. He was upset at himself for not reaching Florida in time to say his goodbye's to her face. He missed the viewing and thus could not take one last look at her.

He, like my father, had not seen his grandmother in years and he beat himself up over it. He had stopped crying as he walked over to me. I hugged him and he began to cry again. I told him I was proud of him because he drove the nearly 22 hours to get here. I also told him grandma was proud of him and that she saw him there and she was smiling. I don't know where these words were coming from, but I meant every syllable. Where was I getting the strength from?

At this point the white box was elevated under a white tent that had a few chairs set up for the final blessing. My cousin walked towards the casket and suddenly threw himself onto the side of it. His face buried in his left forearm, and his right arm swung over the top of the casket he kept saying he was sorry. I got choked up at this raw display of emotion. He really felt like he let grandma down. It was heartbreaking.

I didn't cry at my maternal grandmother's funeral throughout the service in the church. My grandmother meant the world to me, yet I couldn't shed a tear for her. I thought something was wrong with me. Even when my mom cried out that November morning in 2000 that "Mama is dead" I felt overcome with sadness but I did not cry.

I admit it was hard for me to cry. It was hard for me to show emotion especially after my father left. Until this moment writing these words I never thought about why I didn't get emotional as much as I did as a little kid.

I believe the day I broke down in front of my father when I asked him if he was leaving my mother I was very vulnerable. The fact that I was lied to in spite of pouring my heart out may have subconsciously flipped an internal switch on my emotions. I didn't cry much if at all after that. One day my mom hit me and nothing happened. Not one tear. I will never forget the look on her face that day. I was 11 years old.

I got beat regularly as a little kid. Looking back I can't believe I was that much trouble. In my opinion, while I probably deserved the beatings I received, I think my mother really beat me to see me cry. Then when I would cry she would tell me to shut my mouth forcing me to muffle my pain behind quivering lips gasping for air. Then the question that puzzled me the most:

"You want me to give you something to cry for?"

I'm sorry, I thought you already did?

I did not dare say that out loud. This time I took the blow and looked my mom square in the eye huffing and puffing. My mother never hit me again after that.

That was 1990. I don't remember shedding a tear for anything for the next ten years. Yet here I was in Jamaica sitting in the church my grandmother went to on a regular basis, the church where as a three year old running outside I fell underneath a car that was backing out of a parking spot. Trying to get up I kept hitting my head on the undercarriage of the car.

I nearly gave my mom a heart attack. It was her frantic scream that forced the driver to hit the brakes, saving my life. I was not sure if that guy was in the church that day, but it seemed like the whole parish of St. Catherine was.

On the way to the cemetery for the interment I had not cried yet. I was worried. I thought I was disrespecting the memory of my grandmother.

Why wasn't I crying?

When the coffin started to descend into its final resting place, one of my cousins broke through the crowd hysterical. He was not the best behaved of my male cousins to put it very kindly. He gave my grandmother fits during her lifetime getting into fights, stealing, being thrown in and out of jail, but my grandmother always fought for him, always bailed him out, always defended him, always loved him when no one else showed it.

I guess the finality of her death hit him as she was being lowered into the dirt. He screamed her name.

"Mama"! "Mama"! "Don't leave me, mama!"

We were in the middle of the cemetery, but I am sure people walking the surrounding roads heard him. He was loud, he was honest, he was sorry. I am not sure if it was his raw emotion at that moment or seeing my grandmother's casket going into the ground, but my lower lip started quivering, my eyes welled up and it was like someone opened a Johnny pump on a hot summer's day in my eyes. I stepped away from the gathered crowd and let a decade worth of tears out.

I cried loudly. It may sound strange but I was relieved that I was crying. I thought about things in the last decade that I should have cried about but didn't and felt these tears made up for that. If it wasn't for yawning my eyes would get no moisture, my tear ducts would get no work.

The next time I cried after that was in the midst of my conflict with my stepfather. My wife and her grandmother witnessed that meltdown. That was embarrassing. It was not that I felt like I was too tough to cry. I am all for men showing emotion. I was just incapable of it except under extreme circumstances.

So here I was again, this time the voice of reason and calm as everyone cried around me. At the burial site I threw flowers at the coffin already lowered into the ground, I took pictures of the scene:

friends and relatives dressed in black, shades shielding puffy eyes, tissue dabbing at red noses and I was unmoved.

My father had stopped crying and just stood at the edge of the hole that was dug staring at his mother's coffin. His hands folded in front of him, he just stared for a long time. I wondered what he was thinking at that moment: regret over missed opportunity, time wasted not bothering to visit, thinking only of him. It all sounded familiar.

Before I knew it the crowd had dissipated. The gravediggers had started to circle the gravesite ready to start shoveling dirt on my grandmother's coffin. Perhaps it wasn't a coincidence that the majority of the people had left. Maybe I should have walked away too. But I still didn't cry yet. Just like my maternal grandmother's funeral before I had trouble shedding tears.

I wasn't as close to my father's mother, especially when she moved to Florida, but I couldn't forget that she sent a card for my birthday every single year with money in it. When she stopped sending cards she still made sure she called and told me how much she loved me and God bless me.

God definitely blessed me to have two grandmothers as loving and caring as mine. Both passed at the same age of 86. I felt I needed to shed tears for my grandmother. So as the gravediggers shoveled dirt on my grandmother's coffin, I took pictures. Sick ain't it? I was like a paparazzo the amount of pictures I took of every moment.

I stared at the dirt hitting the coffin. With every bit of brown Earth that hit the white box I thought about the finality of everything. I thought about the last time I saw her alive over four years ago thinking that is way too long a time to pass without seeing my grandmother, especially in her condition. I felt shame as well as a breakdown coming. I pretty much forced myself to cry at that moment because my grandmother deserved my tears. She was an incredible woman. It did not mean I loved her any less, I was just frustrated that I wasn't more emotional.

Of course I heard it from my mother, not in a bad way, as she along with my cousins helped me to my feet.

"Come on, Jay. You told everyone else not to cry and be sad."

Yeah, I know what I said. And I meant what I said, but I just feel it is some sort of disrespect not to cry for a deceased relative at some point. I had to let it out. I was grieving like everyone else. Once I pulled myself together... I took a few more pictures. Pictures of the completely covered gravesite freshly packed dirt and all.

After the funeral everyone went back to my grand aunt's house. While there a strange thing happened: my mother, father and uncle among other relatives started talking about the old days. The days I talked about in chapter 7. It got really weird for me because I was in earshot of the flashback conversation. This was the longest I had been around my father in years.

He was on a roll. He brought up the incident where I accidentally put the car in drive. He let out one of his hearty laughs at the memory. He called me "JJ" as he asked me if I remembered. It felt funny hearing my father call me his nickname for me. I was trapped in a sea of conflicting emotions. Was it really all good right now? I wondered how my mother felt hearing these stories while standing next to my father. Does she still feel hurt over how the marriage ended? For a second I thought about bringing the mood completely down; asking why he never came back. Why did he destroy our family and flush all these memories he was rehashing down the toilet?

I thought I was too old to still be bitter, but you never outgrow the dissension felt when someone does you wrong until you set things right with that person. It's okay to reminisce, but don't go down memory lane and act like you didn't do anything to ruin it.

People grieve in different ways. Photo albums were brought out the woodwork and it was just a matter of time until the rare photos pop up. One such photo, a picture of my uncles as little boys, was priceless. For one weekend I had my family back. Too bad someone had to pass away to make it happen.

CHAPTER 17

SCHOOL

They say parents are a child's first teacher. Trey was always very observant. Constantly taking in his surroundings I knew he would be very intelligent. Newborns usually keep their eyes closed for several days. Trey had his eyes open when he was being wheeled through the hospital to the maternity ward immediately after his birth. My mother arrived at the hospital at the same time I was wheeling Trey through the hall. She saw me and gave me a hug.

"Where's the baby?" she asked.

"Right here," I told her as I pointed to the bundle below me.

My mom was stunned to see Trey looking up at the ceiling opening and closing his mouth, possibly foreshadowing the talkative toddler he would become. Whenever anyone held Trey and his eyes were closed he'd, without fail, open his right eye squinting ever so slightly to see who was holding him.

I wasn't surprised when he knew his ABC's as a one year old because when he would cry I would sing it to him. He stopped crying immediately and watched me as I sang. As I looked into Trey's eyes I was amazed that a universal way of teaching letters would captivate him at such a young age.

I knew he would be an active child because he tried so hard to walk. He crawled everywhere. If a child could be an active crawler Trey would be that child. The jumper we bought for him was his favorite piece of equipment because not only could he stand upright as the pouch at his waist held him up, but he could jump around as long as he wanted. I should have taken the hint because he has since turned our bed into a trampoline.

He was so determined to walk I knew it would be a matter of time after he started using the furniture to push himself up. The wall was his crutch as he would guide himself along until a piece of furniture like a sofa or a wall unit impeded his forward progress.

I did not get to see him take his first steps, but I heard about it. Tracy-Ann told me it was as sudden as everything else he picked up on. She called me at work and told me that, while she was on the phone, out of the corner of her eye she saw a small object run past her.

She couldn't believe what she just saw. She yelled out Trey's name and back down the hallway he came laughing as if he just stumbled into a room full of toys, giddy with pride that he was finally able to stand on his own two feet without help. He was still a little shaky only taking a few steps at a time before falling over, but he finally did it.

It was Easter Sunday, exactly a year and eight days from the day Trey was born. When I got home I made a beeline for my camera. Trey was always ready to pose when a camera was around and this time was no different.

"Let's see you walk, buddy," I said.

On cue Trey pushed himself up and started to walk in the dining area. I pushed the record option on my digital camera just in time to catch a few steps before he lost his balance and stumbled forward to the floor.

It was amazing, and no one was more amazed than Trey himself. It was a great feeling. It was also the beginning of trouble. He was active before he could walk, but now that he was able to stand on his own two and really move around it was going to be hard to keep up with him.

****

A few months after Trey's 2nd birthday we decided he should start going to school. He knew his alphabet, how to count to 50, how to count from ten backwards, and how to count from 1 to 10 in Spanish (I had Dora the Explorer and Diego cartoons to thank for that). Without any siblings in the home (even though plenty of people have called our house and heard him in action and thought there were at least three kids playing around), Trey needed to interact with other children.

After researching different schools in Brooklyn we finally settled on a private school that accepted two year-olds. The school had a summer program which was a perfect way to get Trey acclimated to the change of scenery before September. Payment of the registration fee and the accompanying school packet replete with medical forms, uniform and school supplies requirements that arrived at our door was confirmation that our boy was actually going to school.

Reality did not set in until the first day. I was up early. I could not help but think perhaps I had really arrived as a father because of the feeling of extreme joy in something seemingly so mundane as the first day of school. I knew how I felt on the first day of school each year: when I wasn't pulled from the house kicking and screaming, I actually looked forward to the new school year if only to see my friends after a summer gone by.

Trey was eerily calm that Tuesday morning after the 4th of July holiday. He had no idea he would be separated from his parents for the first time in a strange place. As he put on his clothes: (kids did not have to wear a uniform during the summer) an orange short sleeve shirt, jeans shorts and black sneakers, I had my camera ready to shoot his first steps out of the house. Tracy-Ann carefully prepared his lunch and assorted snacks for the first of what would be many times over the next year and a half. The entire morning went by so quickly.

It felt like I was back in the delivery room again. Seeing Trey with his blue book bag draped over his little shoulders and his cap over his head smiling as he looked into my digital camera holding his mother's hand filled me with pride. They say these are the moments a parent should cherish because before you know it your child will be off to college.

It was also important to let him go to school that morning and experience new people. There is only so much my wife and I can teach him. He has to interact with other kids and, most importantly, the teacher. I believe a teacher is an extension of the parents. A good teacher not only prepares a lesson plan, but has a genuine love for children and feels it is his or her duty to take responsibility for educating our youth.

The teacher has to have a personality that can adapt to each child and the instincts to tell when something is wrong. They have to want to gain the children's trust whereas they can confide in a teacher issues they necessarily can't or won't tell their family.

Trey's Pre K-2 teacher was one of those people. She was a God-fearing woman who, although strict with the kids when they misbehave, was very nurturing and hands on. She had such an effect on Trey that when it was time for him to move on to Pre K-3 he kept going back to her classroom. When we drive by the area where the school is Trey still calls her name. That is the impact a teacher should have on a child.

Believe me I have taken in every single moment with Trey. If it is not saved in my digital camera (I still have the photo from his birth stored) it is in the recesses of my mind. No job, besides that of a husband, has been more important to me.

As a first time father I am enjoying every unpredictable moment and milestone. As I look into Trey's smiling face, every time he wakes up singing, or calls me "daddy" I wonder how a man can put himself in the position to be labeled a "deadbeat". As my wife says "it is not about you anymore" and denying responsibility as a father is one of the most selfish acts a man can perform for the simple fact that the child did not ask to be born. It may be cliché, but if you take the time to lay down and create a life, you should be man enough to take care of a life.

I implore all men to step up if you have not already and come back if you have left. There is nothing more satisfying than knowing someone that most likely bears your image looks up to you, wants to act just like you, and follow in your footsteps. It is the best feeling in the world.

That is all.

CHAPTER 18

PROGRESS

I am happy to say that the relationship between my dad and I has improved. The time we spent around each other in 2008 broke down more walls than our initial reunion four years earlier. Although we have not connected for a typical father-son outing we call each other on Father's Day, I call him on his birthday, and he has called to wish Tracy-Ann a happy Valentine's and Mother's Day.

He came to my house during the Christmas holiday in 2010 to drop off a Christmas gift for Trey: an interactive game from Fisher Price that includes a virtual bicycle and teaches letters, numbers, and other tools of learning that he cannot stop playing with. Trey wasn't home at the time of the visit but this was a welcome start.

My dad had called a few times before asking for my mailing address, but nothing ever came for Trey. I was definitely skeptical of his inquiries so I took every call with a cynical approach, not expecting much. However, when he called that day and told me he was in Brooklyn getting a haircut and wanted to know what street I was on I was surprised. He actually showed up.

He came to Trey's 4th birthday party at a Chuck E Cheese in Long Island on short notice with a gift. It was the first time he had seen Trey in person. I was busy playing host, but I did notice that my dad could not stop looking at him. It was as if he was looking at me as a little boy all over again.

Who knows what was going through his mind at that point. I'd like to believe he was reminiscing about years gone by, lost time he cannot get back. It was great to see him with Trey. Tracy-Ann and I were happy he came.

When I speak to him on the phone I tell him I love him when he says it to me, but I still can't call him "dad" yet. Although I am not at that point, I let Trey know that he is my father and his grandpa. I never stopped loving him, but I guess there is still some trepidation there that won't allow me completely let him back in to my heart. You know what they say: baby steps.

I have found that when I'm excited enough to let out riotous laughter, at times it comes out at the same high pitch level as my dad's. While filming Trey play at an indoor amusement park during a school trip, my adlibs resembled something my dad would say when I was younger. It was purely unintentional, something I noticed only when Trey replayed the footage (as he has done almost every day).

I have come to terms with the fact that I cannot outrun my genes. I will always be my dad's son. Certain mannerisms and words are imbedded inside of me. Forgiving my dad has allowed me to accept this.

I have spoken at great length about the importance of fathers in the lives of children, yet it is equally vital that kids respect their fathers. Cherish the moments you have. If your father has been there for you, be there in his time of need when age and the unpredictability of life takes the inevitable toll on the body and mind.

There is also a saying that forgiveness is good for the soul. Holding a grudge against my father and subsequently my stepfather did nothing for me but give me added stress. It is always the best thing to be the bigger person and start the road to repairing a fractured relationship. You cannot move forward if you don't (to quote Jake Shuttlesworth) "get the hate outta your heart". You can't love your significant other and you can't love and raise your children completely.

There are people who have never met their fathers and go on a life-long mission to find their origin. As I stated earlier the need for closure is important. Even if you take a phone call or listen to a long awaited apology from an absentee father, as in life, knowing where you come from can only strengthen you going forward. In my case I made a conscious decision to make sure my son does not go through what I went through. The same goes for my daughter.

A few years ago my wife's grandmother pulled me aside randomly and as she watched Trey play nearby she let me know that it is important that I have a plan to make sure that my son will have something to call his own in the future, a home where he can run around as he pleases and enjoy being a child, and an environment where his parents are loving and affectionate.

While working towards securing property and monetary funds for his future use is definitely a priority, what I can pass along to my kids right now is the knowledge that they are loved every single day. I continuously shower them with hugs and kisses and the smiles I receive in return is well worth it. I cannot fathom walking away from my children the same way I was walked out on. I firmly believe in working out any issues for the sake of the family.

The way I challenge the "deadbeat dad" stereotype is being a positive example to my own son and daughter first and foremost showing I will be there for them whenever they need me.

By being there and remaining visible in their lives it lets them know that they can trust me. That I will be there for them and not let them down. I can teach them humility, not to judge others based on race, religion, or sexual orientation. I can pass on the morals and values I was raised with. I can encourage Trey's love of music and sports (soccer, basketball, and, ahem, bowling). I can foster his love for reading, numbers, and shapes. I can encourage Aja's love of dance. You can never underestimate the power of education and good manners.

Whenever I kiss my wife in front of Trey he breaks out into uncontrollable laughter and tries to push our heads together for more smooching. Aja has the completely opposite reaction. No one can kiss her daddy, even the woman that birthed her.

If you love your spouse and your child(ren) anything can be worked out. Even if the relationship between parents cannot be reconciled, there has to be an effort made to be cordial for the sake of the child. It really makes a difference in the child's development to see stability.

Hip Hop music, like the Black father, has been unfairly criticized and stereotyped at times by those who have not taken the time to learn about the artists making the music. Hip Hop could be said to have been a "father figure" to many youth growing up during the '80s and '90s who identified with rap artists' inner city struggles. The most successful rap artists are the ones who the public can relate to whether it is an artist who has dealt drugs in the past to survive before making it big in the music industry, turned his or her life around after a jail sentence, had issues with family or simply lost a parent. Sometimes successful artists don't have to have a back story. Good music helps, but shows like VH1's *"Behind The Music"* would not exist.

Hip Hop is "family" to these artists and many have passed down the tradition of the culture and their own memories of their experiences in Hip Hop to their own children through advertising, television, film, and music. There are positive young Black men willing to stand up and be fathers in the urban communities of the United States, in the penal system, the Hip Hop industry, and in the film industry.

While I can't divulge whether the recent amount of positive images in movies and periodicals translate into a higher percentage of responsible Black fathers, the fact that there is media coverage that can spark positive dialogue and change the outlook of young Black men towards fatherhood is remarkable. It is time to stop generalizing through use of stereotypes and give equal coverage to the positive young Black men in this country.

Black fathers cannot afford to show any sign of weakness that would make it easy for an outside party to generalize and ultimately stereotype. Truthfully I believe it begins with how our men treat Black women. They are our harshest critics. Treating Black women with respect and without any ulterior motive will go a long way in improving their perception. If Black women feel there are good brothers out there, they will be confident enough to enter into relationships that will be productive, possibly lead to marriage and the beginning of a beautiful family.

I have been fortunate not to have ever lived in a housing project. I was never rich financially, but I am mentally wealthy and I owe that to my mom as well as my dad.

As I stated before my mom was very instrumental in helping me deal with a potentially traumatic situation. Most kids do not have that support system in the home, but why can't someone close to the child – an uncle, an aunt, a cousin – step in and offer a positive word or moral support?

If you believe that athletes and entertainers are role models then men like Ice Cube, Grant Hill, Joseph "Rev Run" Simmons, Denzel Washington, Will Smith, Ken Griffey, Jr. and Jerry Rice are among those who deserve to be praised for being there for their family while taking on the challenges of their respective careers.

A lack of a father figure will either make you succumb to the evils that arise from low self-esteem or motivate you to do that much better so as not to repeat the same cycle of events. It takes a lot of work to pull back the layers of perception and find the diamond beneath the rough exterior. Most people prefer to take a vacation.

Some people feel sorry for themselves and, subconsciously or not, allow negativity to influence their lives. This propensity to do wrong also perpetuates the negative stereotype of young Black men, and while a young man in survival mode is not thinking about what any adult, politician, or pundit thinks about him, someone else has to care in order to begin to reverse the trend.

I love Shakespeare. In many of his comedies and tragedies he wrote about kings. These men of royalty literally killed to have a male child who could carry on their name or be heir to the throne. Black fathers what are you going to pass on to your heir?

Mentors, big brothers, and social fathers where are you? What are you doing to help a youth that is at risk, not even in your neighborhood or community, but in your family?

What am I doing? The book you are reading hopefully is a start.

CHAPTER 19

THE TRANSITION

EDITOR'S NOTE: MERELY A WEEK AFTER THE ORIGINAL RELEASE OF "PASS THE TORCH: HOW A YOUNG BLACK FATHER CHALLENGES THE 'DEADBEAT DAD' STEREOTYPE", I LEARNED THAT MY DAD WOULD BE FIGHTING FOR HIS LIFE JUST AS WE STARTED TO RECONNECT. HERE IS A CHAPTER THAT NEVER MADE THE ORIGINAL PRINT. WHAT I THOUGHT WAS OVER WAS ONLY THE BEGINNING OF THE END...

"Tracy-Ann's expecting again".

"Yeah? That's great, son."

I was excited and I had good reason to be. It was Thanksgiving day and my wife was pregnant with our second child. I was going to be a father again. I was relaying the news to my dad who I had called to wish a happy turkey day.

The lines of communication between my dad and I had been re-opened since that December day in 2010 when he actually showed up to my house, as he said he would, with a Christmas gift for my three year old son, but mostly relegated to phone calls on special occasions and holidays: Father's Day, his birthday, my birthday.

When my dad called to wish me a happy birthday on September 1, 2011 I couldn't believe it. I guess I thought he would have forgotten after all these years. He didn't. A father never forgets. It was the first time in 22 years my dad had a working phone number to reach me.

Still he wasn't as excited as I expected him to be about the news of another grandchild. When my wife was pregnant with Trey I did not get to share the news with my dad, that we were expecting our first child and his first grandchild. That the Samuels name would go on for at least another generation. We missed that moment.

I sensed something was not right.

"How you feeling?" I asked.

After a deep sigh my dad hit me with:

"Not so good, you know. They told me I have cancer."

The nonchalance in which he said this, it took a few seconds for me to process. Then my stomach dropped. No one in my family that I'm aware of ever had an illness remotely close to being terminal.

I was aware of my family having a history of high blood pressure, serious in its own right, but that can be controlled whereas cancer is unpredictable. Too often I've heard about people with cancer who have to go through painful radiation treatment only to have it return. There are also many stories of cancer survivors who continue to lead healthy productive lives.

"Wow. Where?" I uttered. It was all I could manage to say.

"It is in my lower leg. In my bone, but they are trying to contain it before it spread to my upper body."

Damn. I felt a knot form in my throat. I've never heard of anyone who survived bone cancer. My dad had it. How could this happen? To him? He didn't smoke as far as I could remember. It felt like a cruel joke.

To his credit my dad sounded relatively upbeat, like a person who felt this was a minor setback that he could overcome. Yet I couldn't help but feel it was a death sentence.

It was like a bad movie. A father and son who just really started to reconnect and now without warning we could be potentially robbed of all of it. I wouldn't hear of it. The possibility made me sick.

Would he be alive to see his second grand child? He was treating his first like a king. My dad took every opportunity to shower my son Trey with gifts ever since they met for the first time at a Chuck E. Cheese during his 4th birthday celebration.

The way he looked at the third generation of himself it was like he was looking at me all over again. Surely the chance to cultivate this bond would not be taken away.

A million questions began to run through my mind. How long did he know? Who was paying for his treatment? How was he feeling?

After I got off the phone I told my wife who was stunned beyond belief. Not the news we were expecting to hear on Thanksgiving.

I immediately thought to call my mother. It was instinct. It had been over 20 years since they shared living space, but I knew my mom still cared for my dad as a person. He was the love of her life.

As I expected she was taken aback. She was unaware of his condition. My mom usually got her updates about my dad from his sister, my aunt. I guess I got to her first.

"Sorry to hear that," my mom uttered her voice trailing off.

I could tell she was genuinely saddened. Even with my parents' complicated history my mom obviously did not wish bad on my dad.

For it would be my mother who would inform me that my dad was in the hospital shortly after the new year in 2012. I knew he eventually would need to be hospitalized to get proper treatment.

I knew I had to see my dad. Was I looking forward to it? No. He was checked in to Winthrop Medical Center. This information eased my fears slightly for I had frequently seen and heard their commercials on the television and radio about how good their medical staff was in treating cancer patients. Still I never thought I would have to count on that expertise in regards to someone in my family.

I had some trepidation because I wasn't sure how advanced the cancer was and what he would look like. I have seen enough images of how debilitating cancer can be. I did not want to see my dad like that. After all he was still so young.

My wife, bless her heart, stayed on me to visit my dad. Something about not having any regrets if anything should happen to him. I couldn't argue with her logic, but it did not make the trip any easier for me.

I chose a cool Sunday evening in January to make a visit to the hospital, a night I had to work the overnight shift at The Westin Hotel in Times Square. I chose that particular day as an excuse to cut my visit short if it got too awkward or uncomfortable for me. It goes to show how detached, for lack of a better term, I was from the love I felt for my dad so many years ago. My dad was laid up in the hospital with a potentially terminal illness and I was still trying to find an out.

Over 20 years apart will do that. I am certain if we never had such an extended time away from each other I would have run to the hospital the night I found out he was admitted. I just could not drum up the necessary emotion. I wish I could. He was still my dad, but it was not the same.

I spent more than half my life deprogramming any emotion I felt for my dad so his absence would not hurt me anymore. How could I expect myself to reverse that process especially when we have not spent any quality time together since we reconnected in 2004.

He would always tell me "we need to talk", but neither one of us followed up. I surely never reminded him because I was scared of the emotions our talk would conjure up inside of me. The truth was that talk needed to happen if anything to bring closure, especially now that my dad was fighting a life threatening disease. I had to decide if this would be the visit where we would have "the talk".

I found my way to Winthrop Medical Center relatively easily. The facility was huge, an expansive campus of architecturally superior buildings with floor to ceiling windows that rose at least three stories into the air. Maybe an exaggeration on my part, but I knew I had to bend backwards to look at the entire structure.

As I made my way to the reception area I was blown away by how massive the inside of the building was. There were lounge chairs and small glass tables throughout a space that looked like it should be something more extravagant than what it was, if that makes sense. Once I gave my dad's name and was told where his room was I thought about what I would see. I entered the elevator alone and pushed the number 4. My eyes rose to the space above the elevator doors. The silence was deafening. I thought if I occupied my eyes with the continuous motion of the computerized numbers changing with each passing floor I would not have to hear my own thoughts.

I was used to seeing my dad a certain way: physically fit, healthy in the face, but as I stepped out of the elevator all I could think about was the stereotypical "look" of a cancer patient: drawn facial features, emaciated body. You know when you don't want to hear what someone is telling you and you block it out in the most juvenile way possible? "La la la la la la la la la la...". That was the struggle going on in my head.

I made a left turn into the hospital room. The space was relatively small. There were two hospital beds in close proximity to each other separated by an end table. There was another patient on the bed to my immediate left, an elderly white man, definitely not my dad. I continued toward the other bed. I could not immediately see the occupant because the curtain was pulled for privacy.

As I reached the foot of the bed I saw my dad sleeping peacefully. For a split second I thought this was my excuse to leave. It was something about seeing him in this setting, so vulnerable. Still I did not want to run away again. I had been running for so many years and it was time to stick around and, dare I say, talk.

I knew I still had a long way to go in my healing process just in the way I chose to wake him up. I could not bring myself to call him "Dad" as I gently tapped the sheet that covered his legs. I spent about a minute or so repeating the same halfhearted attempts to rouse him to no avail. I stared at my dad contemplating my next move, wondering if I should leave and come back another time

216

seeing as I did have to go to work. I knew I was making excuses again. My dad was possibly on his death bed and all I could think about was going home.

If, God forbid, it was the last time I saw my dad alive I owed it to myself to make sure he knew that I came. I gave one more nudge to his legs and stepped back as he slowly opened his eyes. Since he was on his back his first sight was of the ceiling. His eyes then darted to the left where I was standing. He took a deep breath and used his elbows to push himself upward on the bed.

"Hey, son," he uttered.

"How ya feeling?" I asked.

"Not too bad."

He did not look bad at all. Physically he looked the same. His signature beard was not the huge patch of hair that seemingly swallowed half his face as in the past, but what was left was a scruffy mix of black and gray.

I would love to say that our conversation yielded startling revelations and wild family secrets, but unfortunately none of my burning questions were answered basically because I could not bring myself to ask. I did not feel the time was right, but truthfully at this point would there ever be a right time? My line of questioning stayed along the lines of what the hospital was doing to treat him.

I heard the youngest of the three children he was living with was a constant presence and was assisting with the medical costs. I guess that was the least she could do, right? I have to admit for a fleeting moment I felt bad because I could not contribute anything. I had my own family to provide for. The same way he looked out for himself so many years ago I had a responsibility to the people that stuck with me. I did not feel that for my dad. The truth was if I had it I would give, but I did not.

I took a seat in a chair next to his bed as if I would be staying for an extended period of time. At least that was the plan in my mind. The talk with my dad turned out to be an extension of the phone we had during every holiday. He asked about my family and I told him about Tracy-Ann and Trey. It was the longest I had been around him in one sitting and I don't think I was there more than half an hour.

I started to feel uncomfortable. I told him I had to go to work as I rose to my feet. I guess it was my way to escape before any awkward silence could force me to ask the questions I needed answer to achieve some semblance of closure. I told him I was working the midnight shift in two different places.

"Working hard, huh?" he exclaimed.

"Yeah," I uttered.

"You are my son," he said as he extended his hand to me.

I received his hand and told him to take care of himself.

"Love ya, son," he said.

"Love you, too."

I actually said it. My wife will tell you the "L" word is not one I use lightly. I only say it to a select group of people. I feel it is not a word you say unless you really mean it, yet here I let it go in a small hospital room to a man that I am trying to get away from in my own way once again.

I hated that I was still struggling with my emotions, but I was glad that I still had love for my old man. I did not doubt it, but to say it out loud was huge for me. With that I walked out of the room, onto the elevator, to the main floor and through the glass doors of Winthrop Medical Center. I did not have any immediate reaction to what just occurred. I just knew that I would be back to visit him another day. For now I hope I made his night.

My mom went with my Aunt Allison and Uncle Barry to see my dad on one occasion when his current wife was there. From what my mom told me everyone left the room without a scratch. My mom has long since moved on from those ill feelings she harbored many years ago. As the story goes current wife left the room shortly after their arrival. My dad was happy to see my mom. I wish I would have known they were going to visit. That would have been a scene I would have loved to witness. The last time my mom and dad were in a room together was in 2008 after his mother was laid to rest.

I understand my dad was very talkative that day. He was in good spirits, making a lot of requests that could have easily been taken as demands. Among his wishes: that the youngest daughter and I meet and get to know each other. Supposedly she was in the entertainment field and that was to be our common link. I guess that's how my dad was going to introduce us.

He also wanted my sister to show the youngest girl around the Maryland/DC area because she was moving down there. He wanted my sister to be a glorified tour guide to a woman she never met. Did he really think it was going to be that easy? How many years ago could he have facilitated this and chose to do nothing? Now he was having a moment since he was ill?

I had told myself I would visit my dad again especially since I heard he was making all these demands of everyone. It was like he was giving out his last requests, a verbal will of sorts. This did not sound like the confident man I visited just a few months prior. Had something changed? Was he getting worse? I had to make going back to see him a priority.

I received a few updates from my mom in the weeks that followed and each report was progressively worse. First off he had been moved to another hospital. He was being given aggressive radiation treatments, something that was not happening before. This could only mean that the cancer was spreading. He was not getting better. He would eventually lose his ability to speak due to the treatments. I was told that this demoralized my dad. My mom said he would just stare into space.

From what I gather being able to communicate with family kept him positive. Once he lost his voice he lost his will to live. I had to go and see him. I told myself on my next day off from work I would go back. I did not want any excuse to rush out of the room.

On the morning of April 11, 2012 I was exhausted. I just left my overnight shift at one of the two hotels I was working in at the time. As was customary for me before driving away I sent a text to my wife to let her know that I was on the way home. My cell phone battery was dangerously low. I had forgotten to charge it the previous night and I did not have a charger in my car. I knew I had to get home before the phone cut off. I did not want to be caught outside with no line of communication. My wife was seven months pregnant at the time and I needed to be in constant contact in case there were any complications.

I will admit I was moving a little above the speed limit. The streets were surprisingly free of traffic for a weekday morning. I would be home in no time, I thought. My phone vibrated suddenly. I stole a look down at the cup holder near the gear shift where my phone had been resting.

"Sorry to hear about your pops," the text read.

I swallowed hard. A jolt of nervous energy filled my stomach. I looked at who the text was from and became more anxious. It was my cousin Andre… in Florida. If he was texting me from The Sunshine State I knew something had to be wrong. I did not want to think the worst because I assumed I would be one of the first to know if my dad had lost his battle with cancer.

I picked up the phone and hit the call button on the phone so that it would dial my cousin's number. I did not care if I was driving at that point.

"What's up, man?" my cousin asked with a solemn tone of voice.

"Nothing much," I said. "What's going on?"

"You didn't hear?" he asked.

"No. Hear what?" I hurried.

"Damn, my bad. I thought you knew already."

I knew what my cousin was going to say at this point, but I still wanted to hear the words come out of his mouth.

"Your pops passed this morning."

I immediately felt dizzy. I was still driving at a high speed. My body slouched down in defeat.

"My grandfather told me," my cousin continued.

I immediately thought back to the last few hours during my shift at the hotel if anything weird had happened to me or if I had any strange feelings. No stomach pains, no headache, no crying baby, no connection.

"Hello? Hello!"

I was met with silence on the other end of the phone. I looked at my cell phone and the screen was completely black. My battery had died. I felt like I got hit with a right hook and there was no bell to stop the round, no corner stool to sit on, no corner men to give me water or rub Vaseline on my face. Can you imagine receiving bad news and your only source of communication goes out? I was a wreck. I was still at least 30 minutes away from my home with no one to call to confirm what I was told. I was alone driving with my thoughts.

It was by the grace of God that I made it home in one piece. I quickly connected my phone to the charger and waited for it to return to its normal operation. I knew my phone was back in commission because it began ringing repeatedly. Within the next 20 minutes I spoke to my wife, my mother, my sister, and again to my cousin Andre in Florida.

All expressed their sadness at the loss of my dad, but it was Andre who had words that resonated with me immediately. He told me that he could relate to not having a father around and that I was going to be alright. He said we had to be better fathers to our kids so they do not go through what we experienced. He was absolutely right.

For the rest of the day I was in a daze. I went over my entire life together with my dad in my head. He was the polar opposite of my mother when it came to discipline. While she dealt her brand of tough love, he never raised a hand to me, just his voice. The joy he had when he was bowling and the pride I felt when he was watching me follow in his footsteps. How he guided me on that little red bicycle once I took the training wheels off, to the daring and reckless rider I would become a few years later on my black BMX.

I even played back the near misses we had when he was allegedly searching for me. What if I walked into my aunt's house instead of running around the block? What if I would have demanded more of an explanation at the surprise party in '04? At that moment I stopped thinking about myself. I felt bad for Trey. He would never really get to know his grandpa. At least he met my dad face to face. That is something my daughter will never be able to say. There was not a long time to stroll down memory lane. The following day I was informed that my dad's funeral would be April 15th at Bernard E. Dowd funeral home in Queens. The close proximity of the location to where I recently relocated led me to believe he was living nearby. The irony could not be more cruel.

The morning of my dad's funeral I did not know what to expect. Everything was moving so fast I don't think it completely dawned on me that he was gone. Yet here I was with my wife, mother-in-law, and my wife's aunt pulling into the parking lot of funeral home.

I did not attend many funerals in my lifetime so it was not something I could ever get used to.

As soon as I walked in I was greeted by one of the staff members dressed in a suit. I told him the name of the service I was here for and he directed me to the viewing area. The program that was being handed out had a picture of my dad on the cover from the neck up with the ear piece that had become his signature accessory. The words surrounding his image read *"Service of Homegoing for and In Loving Memory of Neville Beresford Samuels"*. It was official. I walked to the front of the room where I came upon a light blue casket.

The casket was closed. I wanted to see my dad. I wanted to touch him. His other family controlled all the arrangements. I did not know what the costs were to prepare for a funeral, but the way this was set up felt rushed. On the flipside, I knew that he passed away and I did not attempt to assist in making funeral arrangements so how could I criticize? Maybe I expected more from the people that he lived with.

I made the symbol of a cross and stared at the casket for a few seconds. I guess I still could not believe my dad was gone. As I turned to take my seat on the side of the room filled with people that I recognized I could not help feeling disappointed that a large faction of my family, people who genuinely loved my dad, was not here. No one in my family from Florida was represented and that is where the majority of his side of the family lived. I wish they would have been able to come to show that my dad was loved, that he had a full life before he made his decision to live elsewhere.

After taking my seat I began to search the room for signs of his other family. Remember I had never seen these people ever. I had no idea what they looked like or how many people my dad was living with. I decided to read the contents of the program in my quest for answers. A lot of what I read was news to me. According to this program my dad was "affectionately known as 'Nibby'". Now I know for a fact no one in my family ever called my dad anything resembling a Nibby. What the hell is a Nibby? That is not even close to sounding like Neville.

As I continued to read I saw another little known fact: my dad apparently had a trusty "sidekick", his dog Vito. Can't make this stuff up. I kept reading and learned that my dad had five children including my older sister and I. A little quick math told me that there were three children I knew nothing about. For a moment I wondered if any of the three children were biological, but none of them had his last name.

As the program got underway I settled in my seat as the pastor began with a prayer. He then said a few words about my dad. Then he proceeded to ask if anyone wanted to say a few words on behalf of my dad. The program already predetermined who was going to speak. My name was nowhere to be found, but I knew I was going to go up when the time came.

Despite what the program stated there was a long silence after the pastor made his announcement.

I chose to speak after my dad's wife and step kids out of respect, maybe just to hear what they had to say, to get some insight into what my dad was doing, how he was living in those 23 years. However, what I heard were speeches that were short and devoid of substance.

The oldest child came to the podium with a crumpled piece of paper. He was visibly nervous, which was understandable, yet his speech lasted about a minute or two. He struggled with his words despite having it written down. It was painful and awkward to watch. I understand having paper to guide your thought process, but to have your words prepared and only last such a short amount of time did not seem genuine. The man is deceased, you're not introducing him to the stage.

The youngest of the three children was next to the podium. She did not have anything written on paper yet her recollection of her time with my dad did not reveal anything mind blowing. She brought emotion into the room. She began to break down as she reminisced about how my dad would always carry her to school and how he was such a nice person. It was similar to what her older brother shared with the audience, still nothing specific about what he meant to her.

The next person to approach the podium was my dad's mistress. The center of all the chaos, the upheaval, the destruction of my immediate family as I knew it. I straightened myself in my seat so I could get a good look at this woman. She was dressed in all black with a veil covering her face. The fact that she had to be helped to the podium was a precursor to the theatrics to come.

From the moment she began to speak the waterworks came. Through failed attempts to stifle her sobs, she would say that my dad was the love of her life and that she was going to miss him.

Then it was over. That was it. 23 years. I wish I had a stopwatch to time these speeches. I didn't know if she was crying because my dad passed or because she was sorry her gopher was gone. It's insulting, but so were these so-called eulogies for my dad. Three people and no more than five minutes of time combined to pay respects to the man you used for over two decades. The mistress turned wife did not even take my dad's last name (no real complaint there just the principle), but kept that of her youngest child. I had to wonder what kind of arrangement did they have? My mother was still going by the name Samuels or "Sammy" at her job even though she had added the last name of my stepfather 14 years prior.

I felt a bit of disgust at what I was hearing. These people spent over 20 years with my dad and had nothing of substance or relevance to share in his passing. The speeches were as rushed as this wake. To be clear, I never knew what went on in their household nor did I care, but on the surface my dad seemed like he was just going through the motions with these people, a glorified chauffeur whose only purpose was to make sure these people got where they needed to go. What else was I supposed to think when all the kids could remember him for is bringing them back and forth to school, driving one to Chicago. Chicago?

"He loved to drive," said the oldest child.

I'm sure he did if he drove you to Chicago!

There were no personal anecdotes, nothing besides him being a good person who loved sports and was always smiling. These are things I already knew. What was his favorite baseball team? Was he still bowling? These are tidbits that let me know he meant something to you other than a ride to school.

Again, I never met the kids so I had no issue with them, but their mother, the lady who was supposedly married to my dad yet never assumed his last name, the lady who disrespected my mother all those years ago after destroying our family, I definitely had a problem with her. If my dad was happy with the life he was living I would beg to differ.

I grabbed the microphone from the pastor and looked out into the people gathered. The side representing my dad was looking very thin. It was disappointing, but I knew if this was organized a little better my family would have represented. Nevertheless, I was present and it was my time to honor my dad's memory. I did not pull out a piece of paper, I did not have a prepared speech. I felt a moment like this warranted speaking from the heart.

"The first words in my book 'Pass The Torch' are my dad is my hero," I began. I went on to speak about the memories from the ten years I spent with my dad, including the trips to McDonalds every Thursday he got his paycheck.

Then I spoke about how he left. I knew his adopted family was sitting only a few feet away to my left but I did not care. Apparently none of them knew him like I did in half the time. I was going to be specific about my experience with my dad, how he hurt me deeply, yet I was able to forgive him in just enough time to be at the funeral home at that moment.

I recalled the day he left and subsequent days when I realized he wasn't coming back. My words came slow. My voice cracked a few times and I paused at certain times, but only to gather my thoughts. I did not feel the heaviness in my throat which was always an indication that I was about to cry. I am sure my family expected waterworks.

Looking out into the gathering I saw all eyes trained on me except one person: his wife. His mistress back in 1989 could not even look at the son of the man she ripped from his family. Just the fact that she could not look me in the eye motivated me to persist about how destroyed I was that my hero was gone. I continued to work the entire room with my eyes keeping his current wife in my peripheral vision.

I saw my wife dabbing her eyes with tissue. She has been with me for the most part through my entire ordeal. She had a front row seat for all the struggles with my emotions dealing with my dad and my ambiguity about seeing him. She always encouraged me to look for him and put my grudges in the past, something I thought I could never do until I actually had no choice that spring evening in 2004.

My mother was to her left wiping her eyes even with my stepfather sitting right next to her. It was a bit surprising to see my mother's display of emotion during my recollection, but I guess the picture I painted was so vivid it took her back there with me. She went through it firsthand with a better understanding about what was happening. She had nearly 20 years of history with my dad. Before I was even thought of they were madly in love. Married for almost 15 years before everything fell apart.

That is a lot of time invested. Then to spend another 20 plus years with the person he left us for and to remain with her until his death I think hurts me more. He was willing to stay and take care of someone else's family, give that commitment to people that were not biologically related to him yet walk away from people that really knew him, loved him, and appreciated him.

My focus returned to his so-called wife. I will never know what exactly she said or promised to my dad so many years ago to convince him to abandon his family. She still had not raised her head from the floor. I guess hearing me for the first time, seeing me in the flesh knowing what she did I was certain she was dealing with whatever it was: a guilty conscience, karma. Or maybe she was so devoid of any emotion towards us she could care less. Maybe she just wanted me to get off the stage so the program could move on.

Wishing that I stop bringing up memories of the brief time I spent with my dad. Memories of taking me bowling every Saturday, how he taught me how to ride a bike without training wheels catching me every time I fell against a fence or in the bushes. Picking me up when I hit the concrete.

I know my dad had another family out there. I never wanted to think about him having other kids, but here I was staring them right in the face… at his wake. He never got the opportunity to introduce us despite how awkward the circumstances were.

After our reunion in 2004 he always said he wanted to talk to me, a meeting that never happened until that night in the hospital where he had no choice but to see me. I wonder if he wanted to tell me about the three children he inherited, maybe he wanted to apologize, to tell his side of the story, things I really wanted to hear but thought I didn't. Things that would have went a long way in healing our relationship more.

I acknowledged this adopted family by thanking them for loving my dad and being in his life. The shock and awe on each of the children's faces was priceless. Unexpected words from someone who had every right to be bitter and angry. That wasn't me –

anymore. I let those feelings go years before. I actually meant what I said. While the kids were in disbelief that I even spoke of them, their mother still kept her eyes to the floor.

I ended my tribute with the last time I saw him in the hospital, how he told me I was his son.

"Yes, I am your son," I reiterated with emphasis. "Rest in peace, Dad-Neville."

I did not shed a tear during my eulogy. Maybe if his casket was open and I was physically able to view his body I would have reacted differently. I still felt grief. How could I not? A piece of me passed with my dad. Those memories I spoke of are all I have left. The way this service was turning out I started to wonder if his death could have been prevented. From the time he told me of his diagnosis to his death was not even six months. His cancer was full blown. That doesn't just happen overnight.

Whatever I was thinking in private my Uncle Donny said in public. He took the stage right after me and he was visibly shaking he was so angry. My uncle was a pretty laid back guy. I can say I have never seen him upset about anything. Remember he was the only sibling who held it together at his mother's funeral.

However, when Uncle Donny introduced himself as my dad's younger brother his tone was remarkably stern. From my vantage point his grip on the microphone looked like he was squeezing the electricity out of it. Then the jabs came. If my speech was diplomatic, his was no holds barred. Forget how you feel.

"We all make mistakes in life…"

Damn. It did not take a genius to know that he was alluding to my dad leaving his family to play house with his mistress. I mean, it was how I felt as well, but I did not think this was the venue to throw stones. My uncle felt differently and that was his right. The proceedings needed a little dose of reality with all the theatrics going on.

He stood in front of our section of the room, sparingly shooting a glance to the opposite side as he spoke. He wanted answers to questions only my dad could have answered. He wanted his brother back.

I could relate. I felt cheated. Just as I was getting to know my dad he was gone all over again. It felt like a bad rerun, except this time he wasn't hiding in some non-descript house in Queens he was gone for real. Never to return at someone's surprise party or anniversary.

After initially walking out of the funeral home with my family I turned and went back inside. I saw the two younger children, two girls, and hugged both of them one at a time. I don't know why I did it. I owed them nothing. Maybe it was to let them know there were no hard feelings.

"He spoke about you all the time," the middle child said.

"He had your picture on his night stand," the youngest continued. "He cried all the time."

There was a revelation, if it were true. I couldn't see my dad crying over me. If he shed tears it was probably his guilt ridden soul reminding him of what he left compared to what he inherited. It sounds harsh but he was raising another woman's children while his biological son was out there doing God knows what. Looking for guidance, needing to be taught how to be a man. I was robbed of my teacher. I had no concept of responsibility, no direction. While he should have been giving me life lessons he was driving someone else's kids to school.

Do you know how many kids were in the same predicament as I was that have turned to gangs, who are locked up for following the wrong crowd looking for a sense of family? That could have been me wasting away behind bars. And for what? Thank God for Hip Hop music!

My dad should have been crying. How do you reconcile that? As I said before my tears for him dried long ago. It was strange to hear them say they knew of me because I never knew anything about them. He never spoke of them to me at any time. Maybe if I would have stayed a little longer in his hospital room the topic would have come up.

The boyfriend of the youngest daughter took down my phone number. He wanted me to keep in touch.

"You're brother and sister now," he said.

For some reason I doubted we would become this united long lost family. I wanted to tell him that ship had sailed. If my dad could not bring himself to tell me about the people he spent 23 years of his life with why I would embrace them in his passing is beyond me.

She obviously felt the same way because she has not called me. One thing I never do is pretend to like someone. I don't know how to do it. Keeping in contact with my dad's adopted family would not be genuine on my part. It does not mean that they are bad people, but the circumstances are beyond awkward. I would not have the patience to get to know them, especially with the person that links us not around. What would be the point?

To be honest, I did not care about these people. They are strangers to me. I would not know them if they passed me on the street, and they probably did in the past two decades. The hug in the funeral home was enough. Hello and goodbye.

Leaving the funeral home that day it did not seem like I departed a home going service. It felt like another function. As the days and weeks went by it continued to bother me how hastily my dad's funeral was put together. Apparently there was not a lot of input from his side of the family and it showed. The only family members that showed up from outside of New York was my sister and his older brother, my uncle Cliff who both arrived from Maryland.

There was no one from Florida or Jamaica where the people my dad grew up with resided. This disturbed me. Even if they were not invited by his mistress it would have been special to see a huge turnout from the people that truly knew and loved him. Instead there was a smattering of empty seats on our side. I made sure I stayed at the podium a little longer for this reason. The people gathered would know exactly why he was to be celebrated.

EPILOGUE

It has been four years since my dad's passing and with each calendar year that goes by it does not get any easier. I find that I miss him more depending on the day or if something in my personal life triggers a memory. It is especially tough when I hear or see stories on television about fathers being killed by random acts of violence and leaving behind small children.

I am resigned to the fact that I am irretrievably broken. I will never feel the unconditional love for my dad I did as a child and I am finally at peace with that. I am still angry that he was not taken care of. I can't help but think that my mother would have made sure his health was paramount. Maybe that cyst in his foot that he claimed kept him from making an appearance at my wedding was the genesis of the disease that would eventually kill him. Who knows if his condition was taken seriously enough back then to seek proper medical attention. All I could think about at the time was that he was making another excuse not to be around. I never imagined that he could be really sick.

That's what falling out of love does. It makes you become a conspiracy theorist. My family did not have a history of cancer, but when you reach a certain age as a man it makes sense to take your health more seriously. Did he ever do a prostate exam after he turned 50? Men traditionally avoid the doctor or hospital unless they have severed a limb or something, so it would be up to the mistress to insist he take the proper precautions. I'm guessing none of that happened until it was too late.

One thing this entire ordeal has taught me is that I need to make sure that I am healthy at all times. Being there for your kids not only means making a conscious effort to remain in their lives, it is assuring that you are in great condition so you do not have to leave this world before you have to. Whether it is eating healthy, taking the time to exercise be it jogging, taking a walk, playing sports, going to the gym on a regular basis, just keeping active, and getting a regular check up, especially after you reach 50.

My uncle Cliff passed a year and a half after his younger brother. It was October 13th 2013, six days before his 67th birthday. The man affectionately called Boisy would suffer a stroke right in front of his youngest child. It was a shock to say the least. He was the picture of health to the naked eye.

The last time I saw him alive was at his daughter's wedding in September of 2012. He was the same person I always knew: smiling, making jokes, beaming with pride as he watched his youngest marry her college sweetheart. Their oldest and only child at the time was a spitting image of my uncle. It was like looking at a picture of him as a toddler.

He was a devoted husband and father, who did not deserve to leave this Earth in that fashion. Life is short. Death can be unexpected, but it is certain. I still don't have to like it. This was my third funeral in five years after experiencing only one (my maternal grandmother) in 30 years before that. This was a feeling I did not want to get used to. In a final cruel twist of fate my uncle's funeral was on his birthday. His oldest daughter, my cousin Sherry, his only son Clifford Junior and his wife of many years, my Aunt Brenda were among the many family and friends on hand to pay their respects. I knew I had to be there. This man dropped everything to be at anything involving his family. I was happy he was able to be at my wedding.

It would be his youngest daughter Kristina who almost got the waterworks going in me by simply rising to her feet at the cemetery where her dad was to be interred and taking a step towards his casket as it sat ready to be lowered into the Earth and simply saying

"Happy Birthday, Daddy".

Her voice broke off into uncontrollable sobs and she collapsed into her husband's arms. She loved her daddy.

I definitely know that feeling.

Our daughter Aja Emily Sandy Samuels entered the world on June 18th 2012 and she has no idea who her paternal grandfather is.

Don't feel sorry for me. At least I got to know my dad for a decade. Many kids and adults never get the opportunity to spend ten minutes with their father. I can't imagine how empty a feeling to not know who your mother was intimate with. Not seeing wedding photos in a family album or no physical evidence that you were conceived in love.

In a perverse way I think it would have been less painful if I did not know my dad at all from the beginning. There would have been no emotional attachment to suppress in my subconscious. I spent so many years away from him it's like I wiped him out of my memory anyway. In those final years, seeing him was like reuniting with a long lost friend.

The awkwardness of his nostalgic moment after his mother's funeral all the way to the last time I saw him in the hospital, I could not summon anything. The feelings were there. I definitely cared if he lived or died, but that I could not call him dad at the end was disheartening. But I was human. Like anyone that has been hurt by someone you will be naturally guarded with your feelings when seeing that person again.

I never want my children to feel that way about me. That is why I have to do right. That is why I wrote this book. If I do not heal I cannot pass on anything except baggage. No child deserves that. My heart will always be heavy when I think about my dad, but I know he is watching so I must show him that I can do what he couldn't...

Pass The Torch!

Peace and Love.

BIBLIOGRAPHY

Works Cited

Boyz n' Da Hood. Dir. John Singleton. Perf. Cuba Gooding, Jr., Laurence Fishburne, Ice Cube Columbia Pictures, 1991.

Common. *Retrospect For Life*. Perf. Common, Lauryn Hill. Music Video. Chicago, Illinois. 1997.
http://www.youtube.com/watch?v=pmDybzfNBG0

Ed O.G. *Be A Father to Your Child.* Perf. Ed O.G. & Da Bulldogs. Music Video. Roxbury, Massachussetts. 1991.
http://www.youtube.com/watch?v=X7PBeauTvBk

He Got Game. Dir. Spike Lee. Perf. Denzel Washington, Ray Allen. 40 Acres and a Mule Filmworks/Touchstone Pictures. 1998.

Menace II Society. Dirs. Albert & Allen Hughes. Perf. Tyrin Turner, Larenz Tate, Jada Pinkett. New Line Cinema, 1993.

Shakur, Tupac. *Papa'z Song.* Perf. 2Pac *Strickly 4 My N.I.G.G.A.Z.* Interscope. 1993.

The Fresh Prince of Bel-Air; "Papa's Got A Brand New Excuse". Perf. Will Smith, Ben Vereen; television program; National Broadcasting Company (NBC); 1994.

http://www.youtube.com/watch?v=2dS4cxGCpjk

Weinberg, Rick. "Derek and Dad finish Olympic 400 Together"

http://sports.espn.go.com/espn/espn25/story?page=moments/94

Wildeman, Christopher. "Parental Imprisonment, the Prison Boom, and the Concentration of Childhood Disadvantage." *Demography V. 46 No. 2 (May 2009)* P. 265-80, 46.2 (2009): 265-280

APPENDIX

i. Rap Lyrics

EDITOR'S NOTE: THE LYRICS THAT APPEAR IN THIS SECTION WERE HANDPICKED BY THE AUTHOR BECAUSE OF ITS CONTENT AND THE MESSAGE IT CONVEYS AS IT PERTAINS TO THE SUBJECT MATTER OF THIS BOOK ONLY. THESE LYRICS WERE NOT USED OR EXPLOITED IN ANY OTHER FORM AND IT IS NOT THE INTENT TO VIOLATE THE RESERVED RIGHTS OR INTEGRITY OF THE SONGWRITERS AND ARTISTS INVOLVED IN THE COMPOSITION OF THE SONGS. PLEASE BE AWARE THESE SONGS MAY CONTAIN EXPLICIT LANGUAGE.

Artist: Ed O.G. & Da Bulldogs

Album: Life of a Kid in the Ghetto

Song: **Be a Father to Your Child**

http://www.youtube.com/watch?v=X7PBeauTvBk

Be a father, if not, why bother, son

A boy can make 'em, but a man can raise one

If you did it, admit it and stick with it

Don't say it ain't yours 'cause all women are not whores

Ninety percent represent a woman that is faithful

Ladies, can I hear it? Thank you.

When a girl gets pregnant, her man is gonna run around

Dissin' her for nine months, when it's born he wants to come around

Talking that I'm sorry for what I did

And all of a sudden he wants to see his kid

She had to bear it by herself and take care of it by herself

And givin' her money for milk won't really help

Half of the fathers with sons and daughters don't even wanna take 'em

But it's so easy for them to make 'em

It's true, if it weren't for you then the child wouldn't exist

After a skeeze, there's responsibilities so don't resist

Be a father to your child

You see, I hate when a brother makes a child and then denies it

Thinking that money is the answer so he buys it

A whole bunch of gifts and a lot of presents

It's not the presents, it's your presence and essence

Of being there and showing the baby that you care

Stop sittin' like a chair and having your baby wonder where you are

Or who you are----fool, you are his daddy

Don't act like you ain't cause that really makes me mad, G.

To see a mother and a baby suffer

I've had enough of brothers who don't love the

Fact that a baby brings joy into your life

You could still be called daddy if the mother's not your wife

Don't be scared, be prepared 'cause love is gonna getcha

It will always be your child even if she ain't witcha

So don't front on your child when it's your own

'Cause if you front now, then you'll regret it when it's grown

Be a father to your child

Put yourself in his position and see what you're done

But just keep in mind that you're somebody;s son

How would you like it if your father was a stranger

And then tried to come into your life and tried to change

The way your mother raised ya----now, wouldn't that amaze ya?

To be or not to be, that is the question

When you're wrong, you're wrong, it's time to make a correction

Harassin' the mother for being with another man

But if the brother man can do it better than you can,

let him. Don't sweat him, duke

Let him do the job that you couldn't do.

You're claimin' you was there, but not when she needed you

And now you wanna come around for a day or two?

It's never too late to correct your mistake

So get yourself together for your child's sake

And be a father to your child

Artist: 2Pac f/ Wycked

Album: Strictly 4 My N.I.G.G.A.Z.

Song: Papa'z Song

Daddy's home...

[2Pac]

Heh, so??

You say that like that means somethin to me

You've been gone a mighty long motherfuckin time

for you to be comin home talkin that "daddy's home" shit (nigga)

We been gettin along fine just without you

Me, my brother, and my mother

So if you don't mind, you can step the FUCK off, POPS.. fuck you!

[2Pac]

Had to play catch by myself, what a sorry sight

A pitiful plight, so I pray for a starry night

Please send me a pops before puberty

the things I wouldn't do to see a piece of family unity

Moms always work, I barely see her

I'm startin to get worried without a pops I'll grow to be her

It's a wonder they don't understand kids today

so when I pray, I pray I'll never grow to be that way

And I hope that he answers me

I heard God don't like ugly well take a look at my family

A different father every weekend

Before we get to meet him they break up before the week ends

I'm gettin sick of all the friendships

As soon as we kick it he done split and the whole shit ends quick

How can I be a man if there's no role model?

Strivin to save my soul I stay cold drinkin a forty bottle
I'm so sorry...

(Chorus)
I'm so sorry
for all this time (I'm so sorry)
for all this time
for all this time (don't lie)
I'm so sorry
for all this time (so, sorry)
for all this time
for all this time, so sorry baby!

[Wycked]
Moms had to entertain many men
Didn't wanna do it but it's time to pay the rent again
I'm gettin a bit older and I'm startin to be a bother
Moms can't stand me cause I'm lookin like my father
Should I stay or run away, tell me the answer
Moms ignores me and avoids me like cancer
Grow up rough and it's hard to understand stuff
Moms was tough cause his poppa wasn't man enough
Couldn't stand up to his own responsibilities
Instead of takin care of me, he'd rather live lavishly
That's why I'll never be a father;
unless you got the time it's a crime don't even bother
(That's when I started hatin the phony smiles
 Said I was an only child)
Look at mama's lonely smile
It's hard for a son to see his mother cry
She only loves you, but has to fuck with these other guys

249

I'm so sorry...

(Chorus)
I'm so sorry
for all this time
for all this time
for all this time
I'm so sorry
for all this time
for all this time (so sorry)
for all this time, so sorry baby!

[2Pac]
Man child in the promised land couldn't afford many heroes
Moms was the only one there my pops was a no-show
And ohh -I guess ya didn't know
that I would grow to be so strong
Lookin kinda pale, was it the ale oh pops was wrong
Where was the money that you said, you would send me
talked on the phone and you sounded so friendly
Ask about school and my welfare
but it's clear, you ain't sincere hey who the hell cares
You think I'm blind but this time I see you comin, Jack
You grabbed your coat, left us broke, now ain't no runnin back
Ask about my moms like you loved her from the start
Left her in the dark, she fell apart from a broken heart
So don't even start with that "wanna be your father" shit
Don't even bother with your dollars I don't need it
I'll bury moms like you left me all alone G
Now that that I finally found you, stay the Fuck away from me
You're so sorry..

(Chorus)

I'm so sorry (so sorry)

for all this time (so, so sorry)

for all this time (I'm so so sorry)

for all this time (fuck that!)

I'm so sorry

for all this time (no)

for all this time (so sorry)

for all this time, so sorry baby!

[Tupac - impersonating his father]

I never meant to leave but I was wanted

Crossed too many people every house I'd touch was haunted

Had to watch the strangers every brother was in danger

If I was to keep you breathin, had to be out of range-a

Had to move, one to lost my name and pick the number

Made me watch my back I had no happy home to run to

Maybe it's my fault for being a father livin fast

But livin slow, mean half the dough, and you won't get no ass

Hindsight shows me it was wrong all along

I wanted to make some dough so you would grow to be so strong

It took a little longer than I thought

I slipped, got caught, and sent to jail by the courts

Now I'm doin time and I wish you'd understand

all I ever wanted was for you to be a man

and grow to be the type you was meant to be

Keep the war fightin by the writings that you sent to me

I'm so sorry...

(Chorus w/ variations til end)

Artist: 2Pac f/ K-Ci and JoJo
Album: All Eyez on Me
Song: How Do You Want It
http://www.youtube.com/watch?v=ed9yWCPxRvg

Chorus: K-Ci and JoJo

How do you want it? How does it feel?

Comin up as a nigga in the cash game

livin in the fast lane; I'm for real

How do you want it? How do you feel?

Comin up as a nigga in the cash game

livin in the fast lane; I'm for real

Verse One: 2Pac

Love the way you activate your hips and push your ass out

Got a nigga wantin it so bad I'm bout to pass out

Wanna dig you, and I can't even lie about it

Baby just alleviate your clothes, time to fly up out it

Catch you at a club, oh shit you got me fiendin

Body talkin shit to me but I can't comprehend the meaning

Now if you wanna roll with me, then here's your chance

Doin eighty on the freeway, police catch me if you can

Forgive me i'm a rider, still I'm just a simple man
All I want is money, fuck the fame I'm a simple man
Mr. International, playa with the passport
Just like Aladdin bitch, get you anything you ask for
It's either him or me -- champagne, Hennessey
A favorite of my homies when we floss, on our enemies

252

Witness as we creep to a low speed, peep what a hoe need

Puff some mo' weed, funk, ya don't need

Approachin hoochies with a passion, been a long day

But I've been driven by attraction in a strong way

Your body is bangin baby I love it when you flaunt it

Time to give it to daddy nigga now tell me how you want it

(Tell me how you want it! La-dy, yeahhhyeah)

Chorus

Verse Two: 2Pac

Tell me is it cool to fuck?

Did you think I come to talk am I a fool or what?

Positions on the floor it's like erotic, ironic

cause I'm somewhat psychotic

I'm hittin switches on bitches like I been fixed with hydraulics

Up and down like a roller coaster, I'm up inside ya

I ain't quittin til the show is over, cause I'ma rider

In and out just like a robbery, I'll probably be a freak

and let you get on top of me, get her rockin these

Nights full of Alize, a livin legend

You ain't heard about these niggaz play these Cali days

Delores Tucker, youse a motherfucker

Instead of tryin to help a nigga you destroy a brother

Worse than the others -- Bill Clinton, Mr. Bob Dole

You're too old to understand the way the game is told

You're lame so I gotta hit you with the hot facts

Want some on lease? I'm makin millions, niggaz top that

They wanna censor me; they'd rather see me in a cell

livin in hell -- only a few of us'll live to tell

Now everybody talkin bout us I could give a fuck

I'd be the first one to bomb and cuss

Nigga tell me how you want it

Chorus

Verse Three: 2Pac

Raised as a youth, tell the truth I got the scoop

on how to get a bulletproof, because I jumped from the roof

before I was a teenager, mobile phone, SkyPager

Game rules, I'm livin major -- my adversaries

is lookin worried, they paranoid of gettin buried

One of us gon' see the cemetary

My only hope to survive if I wish to stay alive

Gettin high, see the demons in my eyes, before I die

I wanna live my life and ball, make a couple million

And then I'm chillin fade em all, these taxes

got me crossed up and people tryin to sue me

Media is in my business and they actin like they know me

Hahaha, but I'ma mash out, peel out

I'm with it quick I'se quick to whip that fuckin steel out

Yeah nigga it's some new shit so better get up on it

When ya see me tell a nigga how ya want it

How do you want it?

Chorus 2X

[2Pac]

How you want it?

Yeah my nigga Johnny J

Yeah, we out

Chorus

[2Pac]
Tell me

Chorus

[2Pac]
Cash game, livin in the fast lane, I'm for real

Artist: Common f/ Lauryn Hill

Album: One Day It'll All Make Sense

Song: Retrospect for Life

Yo, we gotta start respectin life more y'all

You look at your brother man you gotta see yourself

Gotta see the God within him

Brothers gettin changed real quick over nothin

We losin too many of ours

Gotta recreate y'all

Yo, check it

Knowin you the best part of life, do I have the right to take yours

Cause I created you, irresponsibly

Subconciously knowin the act I was a part of

The start of somethin, I'm not ready to bring into the world

Had myself believin I was sterile

I look into mother's stomach, wonder if you are a boy or a girl

Turnin this woman's womb into a tomb

But she and I agree, a seed we don't need

You would've been much more than a mouth to feed

But someone, I woulda fed this information I read

to someone, my life for you I woulda had to leave

Instead I lead you to death

I'm sorry for takin your first breath, first step, and first cry

But I wasn't prepared mentally nor financially

Havin a child shouldn't have to bring out the man in me

Plus I wanted you to be raised within a family

I don't wanna, go through the drama of havin a baby's momma

Weekend visits and buyin J's ain't gon' make me a father

For a while bearing a child is somethin I never wanted to do

For me to live forever I can only do that through you

Nerve I got to talk about them niggaz with a gun

Must have really thought I was God to take the life of my son

I could have sacrificed goin out

To think my homies who did it I used to joke about, from now on

I'ma use self control instead of birth control

Cause $3 ain't worth your soul

$3 ain't worth your soul

$3 ain't worth it

[Lauryn Hill (two layers of vocals, same words)]

I, never dreamed you'd leave, in summer

You said you would be here when it rained

[Common] Yo

Why didn't you stay

Seeing you as a present and a gift in itself

You had our child in you, I probably never feel what you felt

But you dealt with it like the strong black woman you are

Through our trials and tribulations, child's elimination

An intergration of thoughts I feel about the situation

Back and forth my feelings was pacin

Happy deep down but not joyed enough to have it

But even that's a lie in less than two weeks, we was back at it

Is this unprotected love or safe to say it's lust

Bustin, more than the sweat in somebody you trust

Or is it that we don't trust each other enough

And believe, havin this child'll make us have to stay together

Girl I want you in my life cause you have made it better

Thinkin we all in love cause we can spend a day together

We talkin spendin the rest of our lives

257

It's too many black women that can say they mothers
but can't say that they wives
I wouldn't chose any other to mother my understanding
But I want our Parenthood to come from Planning
It's so much in my life that's undone
We gotta see eye to eye, about family, before we can become one
If you had decided to have it the situation I wouldn't run from
But I'm walkin, findin myself in my God
So I can, discipline my son with my writin
Not have a judge tellin me how and when to raise my seed
Though his death was at our greed, with no one else to blame
I had a book of Afrikan names, case our minds changed
You say your period hasn't came, and lately I've been sleepy
So quit smokin the weed and the beadies and let's have this boy

[Lauryn Hill]
I, never dreamed you'd leave in summer
You said you would be here when it rained
            You said you would be here when it rained
Ohh I, never dreamed you'd leave in summer
Now the situation's made things change
            Things change
Why, didn't you stay
            Why didn't you stay...
I, never dreamed you'd leave, in summer
            In summer
You said you would be here when, it rained
            When it rained, it rained
Ohhhohh I, never dreamed, you'd leave in summer
            You said you wouldn't leave
Now the situation's made things change

Things change, why didn't you stay?

Stay, stay stay stay stay stay stay

Mmmmm, stayyy

Uh-uh

Ohh why didn't you stay..

Artist: **Naughty By Nature**

Album: Naughty By Nature

Song: **Everything's Gonna Be Alright (Ghetto Bastard)**

http://www.youtube.com/watch?v=GTQaocgjLqo

[Intro]
Smooth it out
This is a story about the drifter
Who waited through the worst for the best in crosstown
Who never planned on havin' so didn't
Why me, huh?

[Chorus]
Everything's gonna be alright (alright)
Everything's gonna be alright (alright)
Everything's gonna be alright now (alright)
Everything's gonna be alright (alright)

[Verse 1]
Some get a little and some get none
Some catch a bad one and some leave the job half done
I was one who never had and always mad
Never knew my dad, mother fuck the fag
Where anywhere I did pick up, flipped the clip up
Too many stick-ups, 'cause niggas had the trigger hic-ups
I couldn't get a job, nappy hair was not allowed
My mother couldn't afford us all, she had to throw me out
I walked the strip, which is a clip, who wanna hit?
They got 'em quick, I had to eat, this money's good as spent
I threw in graves, I wasn't paid enough
I kept 'em long 'cause I couldn't afford a haircut

I got laughed at, I got chumped, I got dissed

I got upset, I got a Tec and a banana clip

Was down to throw the lead to any dealin' crackhead

I'm still livin' broke, so a lot of good it would've did

Or done, if not for bad luck, I would have none

Why did I have to live a life of such a bad one

Why when I was a kid and played I was a sad one

And always wanted to live like just a fat one

[Chorus]

[Verse 2]

A ghetto bastard, born next to the projects

Livin' in the slums with bums, I sit and watch them

Why do I have to be like this? momma said I'm priceless

So I am all worthless, starved, and it's just for being a nice kid

Sometimes I wish I could afford a pistol then, though

Last stop to hell, I would've ended things a while ago

I ain't have jack but a black hat and knapsack

Four squad stolen cars in a blackjack

Drop that, and now you want me to rap and give?

Say somethin' positive? Well positive ain't where I lived

I lived right around a corner from west hell

Two blocks from south shit, and once in a jail cell

The sun never shine on my side of the street, see

And only once or twice a week I would speak

I walked alone, my state of mind was home sweet home

I couldn't keep a girl, they wanted kids with cars or chrome

Some life, it you ain't wear gold your style was old

And you got more juice than dope for every bottle sold

Hell no, I say there's gotta be a better way

But hey, never gamble any game that you can't play
I'm slowin' and flowin' and goin' in on and knowin' not now
How will I do it, how will I make it? I won't, that's how
Why me, huh?

[Chorus]

My third year into adulthood, and still a knucklehead
I'm better off dead, huh, that's what my neighbor said
I don't do jack but fightin', lightin' up the streets at night
Playin' hide and seek with a machete sexin' Freddy's wife
Some say I'm rollin' on, nothin' but a dog now
I answer that with a fuck you and a bow-wow
'Cause I done been through more shit within the last week
Than I fly flowin' in doo-doo on the concrete
I been a deadbeat, dead to the world and dead wrong
Since I was born that's my life, oh you don't know this song?
So don't say jack, and please don't say you understand
All that man to man talk can walk, damn
If you ain't live it you couldn't feel it, so kill it, skillet
And all that talk about it won't help it out, now will it?
And illtown fell like I stuck-up props, got shot
Don't worry, I hit by a flurry, and his punk-ass dropped
But I'm the one who has been labeled as an outcast
They teach in schools, I'm the misfit that will outlast
But that's cool with the bull, smack 'em backwards
That's what you get for fuckin' with a ghetto bastard

[Outro]
If you ain't ever been to the ghetto
Don't ever come to the ghetto

Cause you wouldn't understand the ghetto

And stay the fuck out of the ghetto

Why me?

(alright)

Artist: **LL Cool J**

Album: Phenomenon

Song: **Father**

I swear to tell the truth and nothin but the truth...

so help me GOD

I just felt like tellin the story of my life

Felt like, maybe somebody could be inspired, you know?

We all feel pain, we all go through things

But it's time to overcome all that

Verse One: LL Cool J

If your plane crashed in the water and everybody died

would you drown on purpose or try to survive?

I was born handicapped my arm wouldn't move

They called me a cripple pops caught an attitude

Beat my moms smoked lye drove trucks

My moms had a miscarriage, he didn't give a fuck

He sniffed some coke, come home

Beat up on my moms cause she's talkin on the phone

Come on

Chorus: LL Cool J and singers

      (all I ever wanted)

All I ever wanted

      (all I ever needed)

All I ever needed

      (was a father)

was a father

(that's all)

That's all!

(all I ever wanted)

All I ever wanted

(all I ever needed)

All I ever needed... was a father

(was a father)

Verse Two: LL Cool J

Moms got tired of the beatings said, "Yo, we got to go"

Packed up her bags we bounced out the do'

She said, "I ain't takin these whippin's no mo'

I wanna live to see my little Todd grow"

I remember tear drops on my pops face

Lookin down at me standin on the staircase

Handsome brother with a smooth goatee

Makes me wonder why he act so ugly, you feelin me?

(I'm feelin you)

Chorus

Verse Three: LL Cool J

My pops got drunk when me and my moms bounced

Swigged some Jack Dan', sniffed up a ounce

Grabbed the shotty left Long Isle for Queens

Possesed by a demon... a devil it seemed

I was too young to understand the risk

when your moms come home off the midnight shift

She turned around heard the shotgun click

My pops said, "You think that you could leave me?"
He blasted my moms in the back
She fell down screamin I can't forget that
My grandfather tried to close the do'
He got shot ten times in the stomach yo, for real

Chorus

Verse Four: LL Cool J

My head was spinnin, I had never seen blood
Four years old, this don't feel like love
Anyway, pops dissapeared
Grandpops and moms healed up over the years
This therapist got up in her head
Led her to believe without him she'd be dead
You know, they fell in love with one another
Everything seemed right that's word to mother
until I started gettin beatings everday
Sometimes for going outside to play
Late at night on my knees I'd pray
a young child, wishin the pain would go away
Dad where was you when he made me strip
Beat with belts like a slave with a whip
Kicked me down steps outside in the snow
Punched me in the chest stomped me out on the flo'
That's just the tip of the iceberg look
It's too long for a song but perfect for a book
Word is bond, that's real baby

Chorus